Nadia Sawalha & Kaye Adams

Nadia & Kaye DISASTER CHEF

Simple recipes for cooks who can't

Contents

Something for the Weekend

Something Snacky

Something Up Your Sleeve

Something Cheaty

Something Sweet

Something Special

Kaye

If you love food, but you don't love cooking, this is the book for you. And me. And Disaster Chefs everywhere. I have no pretensions to becoming a MasterChef like Nadia, but what a joy it would be to shout "Dinner's ready!" without the kids narrowing their eyes and asking, "Did you make it?"

I'm in awe of Nadia's cooking skills. It's not just that the end result is invariably delicious, it's the ease with which she produces it. I will never cease to marvel at the way she instinctively moves around a kitchen whisking, chopping, laughing, drinking. And more drinking. She is so clearly in her element. I, on the other hand, crash around the worktops like a bad-tempered giraffe on roller skates, constantly re-reading a stained recipe card, cursing frequently whilst hissing at the kids to "let me concentrate!"

The die was cast early on. My mother is a formidable woman who taught me many wonderful things, but feeding a family wasn't one of them. Neither she nor Dad had the time or inclination to be in the kitchen much. My brother and I got by on a hearty school lunch and, for "tea", something-on-toast. As we got older and ate in restaurants, we learned to appreciate good food; just not how to make it.

My twenties were junk-food years, swiftly followed by the fish-finger years when the kids came along – when I also developed my dangerous tendency to improvise with anything I could dislodge from the back wall of the fridge. But it's never too late to learn and I thank Nadia for helping me without bashing her head against the bread board. Much.

What you have here is lots of family-friendly meals and snacks plus a few "ta-da!" dishes, all easy to follow with a bit of extra help on the tricky bits. I also asked Nadia to keep the list of ingredients down. Nothing frustrates me more than choosing a recipe and then finding I am right out of chervil!

And finally, all the recipes have been Disaster Chef tested. Go forth and make a pie!

Kaye Adams

Kaye Adams, Disaster Chef

Nadia

Kaye and I often laugh about when we first met because, quite frankly, neither of us thought much of each other. I thought she was a bit up herself, superior even, and she thought I was a loud-mouthed drama queen with no substance and a lot of hair. I think we were both silently hoping we wouldn't ever have to see each other again…

In retrospect, we were actually both right. And wrong. We did indeed have those unsavoury traits, but we became great friends in spite of them. In fact, I've come to realize, over the years, that our differences are what make our friendship. Kaye loves sport; I utterly despise it. I love to dance on tables; Kaye quite simply doesn't. Kaye loves to ice skate; I love putting ice in my rosé. That's right, dead common, me. Kaye's guilty pleasure is Newsnight; mine is The Real Housewives of Beverly Hills. And, of course, the biggest difference of all: I love (in fact live) to cook… and our very own Disaster Chef does not.

But that's not the whole story. It's not just that she doesn't love cooking; she doesn't even understand that anyone else could like it. For Kaye, being romantic about food is about as daft as it gets. Whereas I can sing songs about perfectly ripe avocados, Kaye's idea of romance with food is mashing a potato (badly).

So, as far as I'm concerned, I'm on a mission with this book to help those of you who are just like Kaye. I can't bear the thought that there are thousands of you out there who, night after night, have to gird your loins, take a deep breath, and force yourselves to create (or cremate) something to feed your family. Disaster Chefs of the world, fear not! A MasterChef is here, riding on a white steed to try and take the pain away. Contained herein are more than 80 recipes, specially designed with this premise in mind: if Kaye can cook it, you can cook it!

Nadia Sawalha ♡

Nadia Sawalha, Celebrity MasterChef Champion

Something to Get You Started

KAYE: When Nadia suggested including instructions for how to make the perfect boiled egg in this book, I thought she was having a laugh. I might be a self-confessed Disaster Chef, but even I know how to boil an egg! And I have churned out mountains of mashed potato in my time, not to mention a few gallons of cheese sauce.

But I have to concede that seldom do these basics turn out the same every time. Some nights, the gods conspire to help me produce wonderful, creamy mash. Other nights, it's grey and lumpy, worthy of a bit part in *Prisoner: Cell Block H*. Sometimes, my egg is gloriously runny. Other times, it could leave an egg-shaped hole in a double-glazing unit.

What I have realized, over the many happy nights I have spent twiddling a glass of wine while Nadia cooks, is that she seems to instinctively know a whole load of tips and tricks that have just passed me by.

It was a revelation to me to learn you should dry tatties off before mashing, for instance, or warm the milk before you make a cheese sauce, or even turn off the heat under a saucepan and set a stopwatch to get the same results for a boiled egg every single time.

It's not rocket science, as they say, but it is crucial to learn the basics and apply them. I guess it's the cooking equivalent of learning to walk before you can run.

If you don't want to be a Disaster Chef all your life, this chapter is a very good place to start.

Essential Gadgets

NADIA: Kaye's cutlery drawer used to put me in a place of abject misery. Blunt knives, rotting wooden spoons, and melted plastic spatulas were the only things I could ever find. Her cupboards were no better. Dark, sad caverns packed full with next-to-useless old tins, all bent up, smashed, and rusty.

A graveyard of OAP frying pans, every one of them with wonky melted handles like a Salvador Dalí painting, and, most terrifyingly of all, peeling Teflon (I swear her daughters and her hubby must all have stomachs lined with Teflon, because there's none left on her pans.)

After many attempts to get her to throw them all out and start again, I eventually gave up and did it myself. I can tell you she was not happy! She kept muttering that her battered pans and utensils had character. So, being the pretty-damn-near-perfect mate that I am, I replaced them all with spanking brand-new pots, pans, and gadgets. So pristine was her new kitchen clobber that you needed sunglasses to enter the room.

But this wasn't just an act of generosity and culinary benevolence, no, I went the extra yard for Kaye because secretly I know that, deep in her heart, she really does want to be a good cook. And without some solid equipment (and a certain cookbook – in fact, the one in your hands), she was never in with a chance.

A good pair of digital scales

Believe it or not, Kaye has traditionally used her eye to "weigh" ingredients, which makes me think she must be short-sighted and long-sighted in equal measure.

An oven thermometer

If your oven is as dodgy as Kaye's, think about buying one, as it's tricky to bake when you don't know the actual oven temperature!

A food processor

A wonderful thing if you are time-poor; it will grate, mix, and chop in seconds for you. We are still waiting for one that makes a perfect gin and tonic.

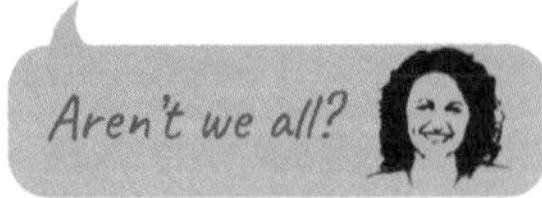

A sharp potato peeler

Kaye's was so blunt that, when I ran it over my tongue, I didn't feel a thing.

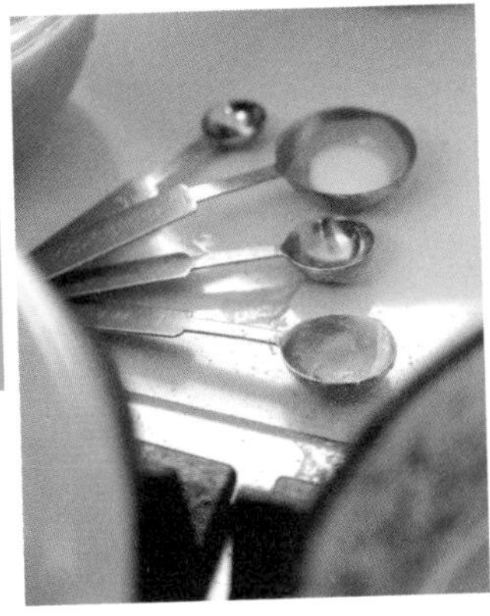

An electric hand whisk

Life's too short to stand whisking meringue by hand, eh, Kaye?

A stainless-steel hand whisk

Kaye's was a bright green plastic one from her home economics class back in 1951...

A silicone pastry brush

Kaye's 25-year-old bristle brush was harbouring so much bacteria that a health and safety officer would have shut her kitchen down. And there were just five bristles left.

A heat diffuser

Everything Kaye cooked on the stove was burnt before I got her one of these.

A mandoline

For slicing things super-thinly. When I told Kaye I'd got her one of these, she said, "I'm too old to learn how to play an instrument!" It's not an instrument. It slices things. Really thinly.

A garlic crusher

Kaye's family quite literally got down on bended knee and thanked me for this – no more lumps of raw garlic!

A Microplane

For grating Parmesan and any kind of citrus zest. No, you don't need a pilot's licence, Kaye.

A spring-loaded apple corer

These are brilliant because you don't have all that nonsense of trying to get the cores out with a variety of ever-more-dangerous implements.

A spiralizer

It took Kaye three months to decide to pay out for one of these – three months! – but now she spiralizes everything she lays her hands on...

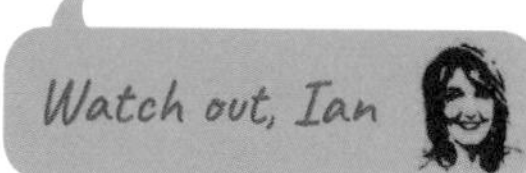

Perfect Boiled Eggs

Makes 2

NADIA: Some may say it's a bit of an insult to put a recipe for boiled eggs in a cookery book… But this method is rather clever and, as long as you have a stopwatch on your mobile, it's foolproof. And an actual chef taught me how to do this!

2 eggs
salt
Twiglets, to serve (optional)

Hack

The eggs should be at room temperature, to help prevent cracking.

1 Bring a saucepan of water to the boil until you have big popping bubbles, not funny little ones. Salt the water to help seal the eggs if they crack.

2 Put an egg onto a spoon and gently lower it into the water. Repeat for the other egg.

3 Reduce the heat to a simmer and cook for exactly 1 minute. Now turn the heat off.

4 Put the lid on, set the stopwatch on your mobile, and leave for:
4 minutes: runny yolk, wobbly white
6 minutes: not-as-runny yolk, firm white
12 minutes: hard-boiled

5 I serve this with Twiglets. Don't knock it until you've tried it.

I've only just found out that you're not meant to keep eggs in the fridge – so what are you supposed to do with the little egg holders in the door, are they for chocolate oranges?

Perfect Mash

Serves 4

NADIA: Kaye says every time she makes mash it is a game of Russian roulette: it could be OK, but it could be awful. Follow these tips and it will be perfect. I haven't said to use a ricer because I don't get on with them, but feel free to if you prefer!

Can I use any old potato?

No, use Maris Piper, King Edward or Yukon gold potatoes (not Red Desirée, as they won't break up well)

900g (2lb) potatoes
1 tsp salt
100g (3½oz) unsalted butter
50ml (1¾fl oz) milk
freshly ground black pepper

1 Cut the potatoes into equal-sized pieces and put in a big saucepan. Cover with cold water and add the salt.

2 Bring to the boil, then reduce the heat to a simmer and cook for 20–25 minutes, testing to see when they're tender with the tip of a sharp knife.

3 Drain very well, return the potatoes to the pan, and set over a very low heat for a minute to dry off.

4 Add the butter, milk, a little more salt, and some pepper, then mash with your masher until smooth.

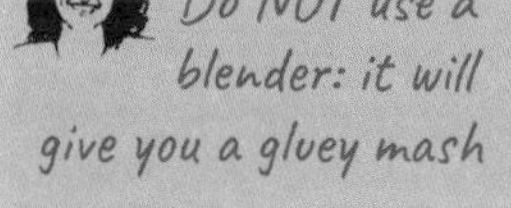

Do NOT use a blender: it will give you a gluey mash

Moisture is the death of good mash!

Hack

When you're boiling potatoes, always start with cold water. This way, the potatoes and water heat up at the same time, so the spuds will cook evenly.

Equal sizes, cold water, dry the potatoes... couldn't someone have told me this 30 years ago?

Perfect Cheese Sauce

Makes enough for a cauliflower or macaroni recipe for 4

KAYE: I learned to make cheese sauce in home economics class some time before Parmesan was discovered in Scotland. It had a rather grey tinge. So Nadia's recipe is now my go-to. I took a lot of convincing to warm the milk rather than grab it out of the fridge, but it does make a difference.

Don't use a non-stick saucepan: the whisk will scratch the coating into your sauce

50g (1¾oz) unsalted butter
50g (1¾oz) plain flour
600ml (1 pint) warm milk
100g (3½oz) mature Cheddar cheese, grated
50g (1¾oz) Parmesan cheese, grated
salt and freshly ground black pepper

1 Melt the butter in a saucepan over a medium heat. Add the flour and whisk it briskly with a balloon whisk.

2 Slowly pour in the warm milk, whisking constantly. Once the mixture thickens, reduce the heat to very low and let it simmer for 5 minutes.

3 Add both cheeses and stir until melted and smooth. Season with salt and pepper to taste.

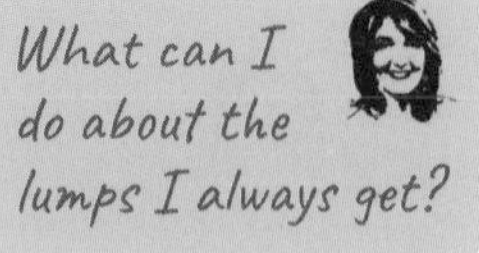

What can I do about the lumps I always get?

Keep the faith and carry on whisking until the sauce becomes smooth

Hack

If your sauce base is still lumpy after you've whisked in the flour, simply press it through a sieve into a clean saucepan.

To avoid lumps, warm the milk and add it s l o w l y.

Perfect Rice

Serves 4

NADIA: There are so many different ways to cook rice, but this is the method I was brought up with and it has always worked for me. You can leave the rice like this, lightly covered, for up to 1 hour before serving, if it's more convenient.

240ml (8fl oz) basmati or jasmine rice
1 tsp salt

1 Put the kettle on to boil. Measure the rice in a measuring jug, then pour into a non-stick or cast-iron pan with the salt.

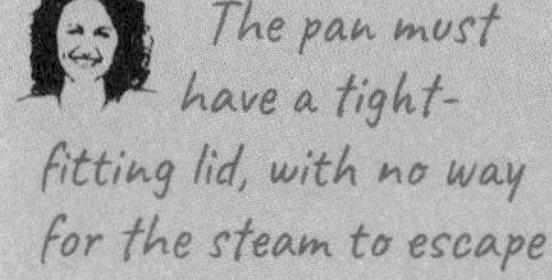

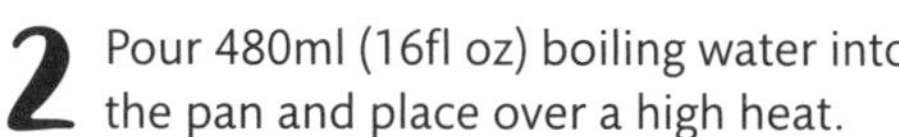

2 Pour 480ml (16fl oz) boiling water into the pan and place over a high heat.

3 As soon as the water returns to the boil, stir the rice once and put the lid on.

4 Reduce the heat to very low and cook for 15 minutes. Do not uncover the pan.

5 If you don't want to eat it straight away, remove the lid and cover with a clean tea towel or a sheet of kitchen paper. It will be OK for up to 1 hour.

Oh, how I have resisted this method of making rice. The stroppy teenager in me wants to chuck some rice in, chuck some water in, and boil it up. And that is why I have spent most of my life eating lumps of rice the size of tennis balls. So if you prefer your rice light and fluffy and grain-by-grain, do what the lady says

Perfect Burgers

Serves 4

KAYE: I have to fight hard against my instinct to buy a pack of burgers that some nice person has already prepared. However, my meat-eating family assures me that these taste like no shop-bought burgers and it suits me, as I can make them the night before and have dinner ready in 15 minutes. Win-win.

Do not pound the meat: if it's overworked, it will be dry

4 tbsp sage and onion stuffing mix
500g (1lb 2oz) minced beef
50ml (1¾fl oz) Guinness
½ tsp salt
freshly ground black pepper
burger buns, to serve (optional)

Can I use lean minced beef?

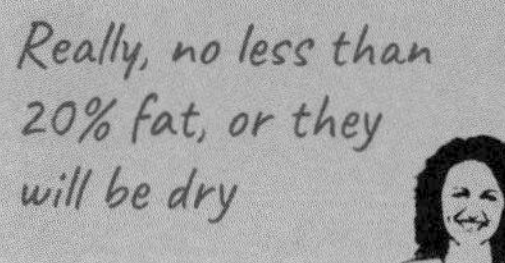

1 Mix the stuffing in a large bowl with 6 tbsp boiling water and allow to cool completely, then add the beef and Guinness. Season with the salt and pepper, and mix with your hands.

2 Gently pat into 4 even-sized burgers. Make an indent in the middle of each patty.

This keeps them flattish and prevents them from balling up when you cook them

3 Ideally you should cover these now and pop them in the fridge for 1 hour, but I don't usually have time. I'm allowed to go against my own advice.

4 Now heat your barbecue, griddle pan, or grill to nice and hot.

5 Put your burgers on the barbecue or griddle pan, or under the grill for at least 3 minutes, then flip them and cook the other side until done to your liking.

Do not move, prod or prick them

6 Eat on your bun – or not – with lettuce leaves, tomato slices, and red onion rings, if you fancy, or with no toppings at all, if that's how you roll.

Hack

If you make doll-sized burgers, they go down a treat at kids' parties.

Perfect Steak

Serves 4

KAYE: A perfect example of a simple dish Nadia does instinctively but I struggle with. I am only prepared to see so many steaks scraped into the bin. So, read her instructions twice and follow them. Eventually, it becomes second nature, which is a huge buzz.

4 steaks – try and get them at least 2cm (¾in) thick and of an even thickness: my favourite is sirloin, Mark's is fillet)

a little olive oil

sea salt and freshly ground black pepper

50g (1¾oz) unsalted butter

½ garlic clove, crushed

handful of flat-leaf parsley leaves, finely chopped

Hack

If you use a thermometer:
Rare = internal temperature of 55–60°C
Medium = internal temperature of 65–70°C
Well done = internal temperature of 70°C

If you use a finger or tongs:
Rare = soft when pressed
Medium = springy when pressed
Well done = very firm when pressed

1 Take the steaks out of the fridge a couple of hours before you're going to cook them, so they can come to room temperature. Pat them dry with kitchen paper. Keep them covered and away from pets.

2 Put a large frying pan or griddle pan over a medium-high heat and leave it to heat up. If you haven't got a large pan, use 2 smaller pans. Do *not* overcrowd the pan, as this reduces the heat and the meat will release juices and begin to stew.

3 Brush both sides of the steaks with a little oil and sprinkle them with salt and pepper, again on both sides.

4 Put the steaks into the hot pan or griddle and cook for 3 minutes. They should sizzle as they hit the pan. Do not touch them, poke them, prod them, or move them. Once beads of moisture appear on the first side, turn them over using a spatula or tongs. Cook for another 3 minutes for medium-rare.

Only turn your steak once; the more you flip it, the tougher it gets

5 Take the steaks out of the pan and keep them warm. Always rest steaks for 2–4 minutes before serving.

6 Reduce the heat under the pan to low and throw in your knob of butter and the garlic.

7 Stir until the garlic is *just* brown. Stir in the parsley, then drizzle the butter over the steaks. Season again and serve.

No more, or the garlic will burn and taste disgusting

Something for Everyday

KAYE: I'm assured there are people out there – and Nadia is one of them – who like to unwind at the end of the day by preparing an evening meal. Can I tell you the truth? Most nights, I would rather stick pins in my eyes.

Cooking is just one more thing to do in between the homework, running the kids to (or picking them up from) their various clubs, sticking on a wash, walking the dog, answering emails, and so on, and so on.

And then I have to consider who will eat what. I am a fish-eating veggie. Ian and the kids are rampant carnivores. The youngest can sniff out a vegetable at 100 paces, while her teenage sister keeps to her own schedule and expects 24-hour kitchen service. Yes, I know the perfect family sits down at 6pm and everyone eats the same thing, but it doesn't happen in our house.

I'd love to say I plan my menus every week, but you wouldn't believe me anyway. What I do is a big online shop with a vague idea of doing something chickeny, something fishy, something meaty, a pasta, and some veggie stuff. My order arrives on Monday morning and I stand and look at it for about 20 minutes thinking, "What am I going to do with this lot?"

Thankfully, Nadia has swooped to the rescue with these recipes: easy-to-make, great-tasting meals for all the family, using just the regular stuff you've got in the house. Even I might enjoy making them.

Something Chickeny

Sweet & Sour Chicken

Serves 4

KAYE: I've just served this to my two girls. My eldest is a bit of a foodie and she gave me the highest compliment I could wish for: "It's better than M&S." Result.

It's important that the pieces of chicken are all the same size: that way, if one is cooked, you know they all will be

For the sauce

- 1–2 tbsp runny honey (2 is yum, 1 is healthier)
- 2 tbsp cider vinegar
- 2 tbsp soy sauce
- 1 tsp garlic powder
- ¼ tsp salt
- 2 tbsp tomato ketchup
- 200ml (7fl oz) pineapple juice (see below; top up with water if there's not enough)
- 2 tbsp cornflour mixed with 1 tbsp water

Don't be alarmed if it looks a bit weird... it does, but keep mixing, it goes smooth

I never get alarmed when things look weird. I am used to it

For the rest

- 2–3 tbsp cornflour
- 3 skinless and boneless chicken breasts, cut into 3cm (1¼in) chunks
- 2 tbsp coconut or vegetable oil, plus extra for cooking the pepper
- 432g can pineapple chunks in natural juice, drained, and juice reserved (see above)
- 1 green pepper, deseeded and thinly sliced (optional)
- Perfect Rice (see p17), to serve

Not olive oil; it can't get to a high enough heat without burning

1 Put all the sauce ingredients in a non-stick saucepan, bring to the bubble while stirring until glossy and thickened, then simmer over a very low heat (or turn the heat off) until the chicken is ready.

2 Put the cornflour and some salt in a large plastic sandwich bag, add the chicken, and give it a good shake until all the chicken is totally coated.

3 Heat the oil in a large wok or frying pan, bringing it up to heat slowly until it's nice and hot. Fry the chicken, in batches if necessary, over a medium heat for 2 minutes, until light golden, then turn over and cook for another minute. Using a knife, check if the inside is cooked through. Remove with a slotted spoon to a warm plate.

4 Add the pineapple to the sauce to warm through, gently reheating over a low heat if you turned it off earlier. Splash in a little water if the sauce is thicker than you want.

5 Meanwhile, wipe out the wok with kitchen paper, add a little more oil, then stir-fry the green pepper (if using) for a couple of minutes until slightly softened.

6 Take the sauce off the heat and add the pepper, then pour over the chicken. Serve with Perfect Rice and steamed broccoli... or whatever green veg you can get your little darlings to swallow.

Chicken Tray Bake

Serves 4

NADIA: OK Kaye, I admit this dish does need a little longer than the 20 minutes you demand everything takes, but you can pop this one on and then go and write emails, play on the zip wire, dance naked in the rain, have a cuddle with Bea (her dog)...

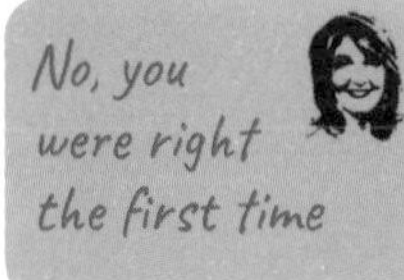

- 600g (1lb 5oz) new potatoes, unpeeled and halved
- 2 onions, sliced
- 4–6 garlic cloves, halved, but leave the skins on
- salt and freshly ground black pepper
- 3 tbsp olive oil, or as needed
- 8 chicken thighs, skin on and bone in
- 20 cherry tomatoes
- 150g (5½oz) good-quality pesto

Faff alert

Kaye would rather stab hot needles in her eyes than brown the chicken skin. But, if you fancy it, just heat a frying pan over a medium heat at the end of step 2. Rub a little oil and salt onto the chicken skin, and fry until lightly golden.

1 Preheat the oven to 200°C (400°F/Gas 6). Put the potatoes, onions, and garlic into a large baking tray and season well with salt and pepper.

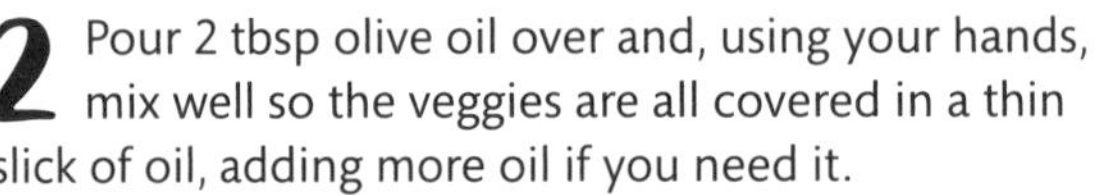

2 Pour 2 tbsp olive oil over and, using your hands, mix well so the veggies are all covered in a thin slick of oil, adding more oil if you need it.

3 Now arrange the chicken thighs on top and drizzle the remaining oil over them. Season and rub in.

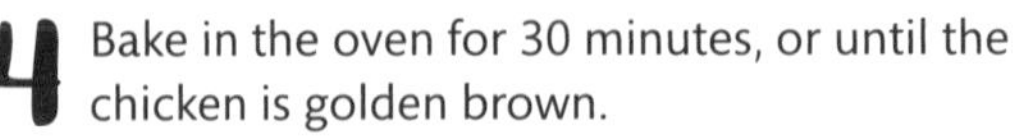

4 Bake in the oven for 30 minutes, or until the chicken is golden brown.

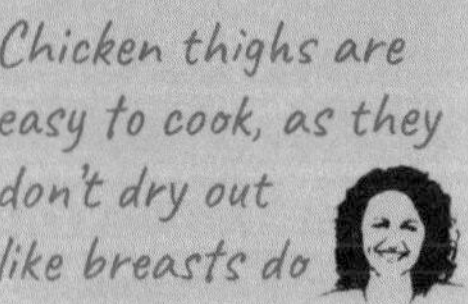

5 Remove from the oven and add the tomatoes to the tray. Give everything a turn, then return to the oven for a final 10 minutes.

6 In a teacup, mix the pesto with 2 tsp boiling water to loosen it, then drizzle it over the dish.

7 Dinner's ready!

What's the point of a tray bake if you have to wash 2 pans?

If you use a flameproof baking tray, you can brown the chicken in it

Peanut Butter Chicken

Serves 4

NADIA: This is cheat's satay, a dinner using just six ingredients: even your teenagers could easily knock this up. Kaye and I are both peanut-butter addicts and I will often find tell-tale finger marks in pots of mine, after Ms Adams has left the building.

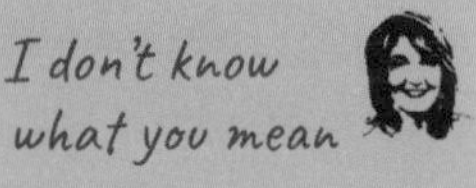

I don't know what you mean

- 1 lime
- 4 tbsp crunchy peanut butter
- 4 skinless and boneless chicken breasts
- 3 tbsp light soy sauce
- a little sunflower oil, for the tin
- 2 x 250g packets pre-cooked rice, or Perfect Rice (see p17)
- small bunch of chives
- grated raw carrot, to serve (optional)

1 Preheat the oven to 200°C (400°F/Gas 6).

2 Zest the lime into a bowl using a zester to get fine strips, then add the lime juice and peanut butter, and stir to mix well.

If I am allowed to give a bit of advice, I stick the peanut butter in the microwave for a few seconds to make it easier to spread

Hang on, I give the advice round here!

What's the difference between light and dark soy sauce?

Light soy is thin and salty; dark is thicker, sweeter and – erm – very dark in colour!

Slash the chicken so the marinade has the chance to get to work quickly

3 Make a couple of deep slashes in each chicken breast. Massage in the lime and peanut mixture, then pour over the soy sauce and mix.

4 Place the chicken in a snug-fitting, well-oiled baking tin.

Continued >>

5 Pop into the oven for 15 minutes. Turn the chicken over, add 5 tbsp water, and shake the tray to make sure nothing is sticking. Pop back in the oven for another 5–10 minutes, or until cooked through. Once the chicken is cooked, if using pre-cooked rice, heat up the rice according to the packet instructions.

6 Meanwhile, lift the chicken out of the tin and put onto 4 warm plates, spooning over some of the sauce.

7 Empty the rice into the baking tin. Using a pair of scissors, snip the chives into the rice and give it all a good stir, making sure the rice absorbs the lovely chicken cooking juices.

8 Divide the rice between the plates and serve to your little darlings, with piles of grated raw carrot, if you like.

HACK
Pescatarians like Kaye can substitute prawns for chicken.

Spanishy Garlicky Sherryish Chicken

Serves 4

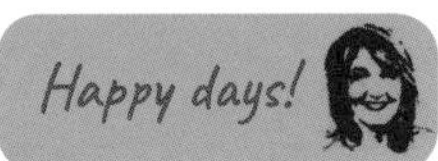

NADIA: Every New Year, Kaye and I and our families get together in Spain and stuff our faces, drink too much, and take long walks on the beach. Every time we eat this dish, we are transported back.

- 3 tbsp olive oil
- 2 onions, sliced (red are nice here)
- 6–10 garlic cloves (you don't have to peel them if you can't be bothered)
- 2 peppers, different colours, deseeded and sliced
- 2 tbsp smoked sweet paprika
- 300ml (10fl oz) dry sherry
- 8 skinless and boneless chicken thighs
- 10 mushrooms, sliced
- salt and freshly ground black pepper
- 2 bay leaves

Faff alert

To make it look really professional, sprinkle with chopped parsley and finely grated orange or lemon zest.

1 Heat the oil in a large lidded pan and throw in the onions, garlic, and peppers. Cook over a medium heat for 4–5 minutes until softened.

2 Now stir in the paprika, pour in the sherry, then bring to the boil for 30 seconds. Drop in the chicken and mushrooms.

3 Season well and add the bay leaves, then pour in 100ml (3½fl oz) water.

4 Bring up to the bubble, then reduce the heat to very low. Cover and cook for 20–25 minutes, or until the chicken is cooked. Remove the bay leaves. Squash the garlic cloves into the pan to release all the flavour, removing their skins if you left them unpeeled. You will have a thin sauce and that's the way it's meant to be.

Cut into a piece to check: it should have no trace of pink

Garlicky Herby Chicken Nuggets

Serves 4

KAYE: Making sure everything is cut into equal sizes, and not overcrowding the tray, are like biblical revelations to me. Before I cottoned on to those two simple rules, my nuggets looked like the aftermath of a wildfire. Now, my children walk past those Golden Gates to get to them. Hallelujah! You will need some spray oil.

- vegetable oil, for the trays
- 150ml (5fl oz) whole milk
- squeeze of lemon juice
- 4 skinless chicken breasts, cut into even nugget-sized chunks
- 125g (4½oz) fine dried breadcrumbs
- 2 tbsp garlic granules
- 1 tsp onion salt
- 2 tbsp dried oregano, or thyme, or finely chopped parsley leaves
- finely grated zest of 1 lemon
- 1 tbsp sesame seeds (optional)
- salt and freshly ground black pepper
- vegetable spray oil

Hack

You can make a big batch of these and freeze them raw if you want. Just put them in the freezer on a tray (so that they freeze separately rather than in a clump). When frozen, transfer to a freezer bag and seal. These cook from frozen in 35 minutes. Use within 3 months.

1 Preheat the oven to 190°C (375°F/Gas 5). Oil 2 baking trays and put them in the oven.

2 Mix together the milk and lemon juice. It will go all lumpy and yucky-looking; don't worry, it's supposed to. Put the chicken in a bowl and pour the milk and lemon juice mix over it. Set aside.

3 Mix together on a plate the breadcrumbs, garlic, onion salt, oregano, lemon zest, and sesame seeds (if using). Season with salt and pepper.

4 Take the chicken pieces from the bowl and roll them in the breadcrumb mix until they are completely covered. Then lay them on the hot baking trays, leaving space between each, and spray with oil, then turn over and spray the other side.

5 Bake for 20–25 minutes, turning halfway. To test for doneness, put a sharp knife through the middle to check there is no trace of pink.

Why do you soak the chicken – it seems like a faff?

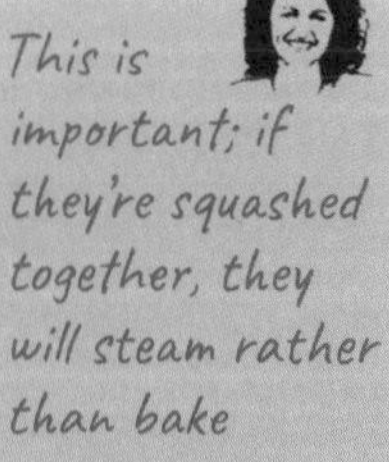

Date and label the freezer bag!

I always do... NOT

Something Meaty

Sticky Sausage & Onion Bake

Serves 4

KAYE: We all need one of these recipes in our lives: we're knackered, so we bung it on a baking tray and into the oven. Low-effort, but everyone loves it. Don't bother peeling the potatoes. Use the three minutes you'd have wasted doing that to pour yourself a gin and tonic.

- 6–8 mini peppers
- 1 red onion, fairly thinly sliced
- 2 potatoes, cut fairly small, no need to peel
- 2 tbsp olive oil
- salt and freshly ground black pepper
- 8–10 good-quality sausages
- 2 tbsp runny honey

You don't want lots of yucky fat pouring out of them!

You can make this with veggie sausages as well, just follow the packet instructions for how long to cook those

Hack

This can be kept in a low oven for up to 1 hour if the family is home at different times.

1 Preheat the oven to 230°C (450°F/Gas 8).

2 Put all the vegetables in a baking tray and drizzle the olive oil over them, then, using your hands, toss them so they are covered in oil. Sprinkle with salt and pepper.

3 Lay the sausages on top.

4 Put in the oven for 25 minutes, then remove from the oven, turn everything over, and drizzle the honey over the top.

5 Return to the oven for another 20 minutes. Dinner's ready!

Pork Chops, Apples & Cider

Serves 4

NADIA: Pork chops are notoriously difficult to get right, but that's often because the meat isn't that great to start with. My advice? Have these as a treat; ditch the supermarket in favour of a butcher and buy the best meat you can afford. There will be plenty of fat – very important for the tastiest flavour, and you can cut it off on your plate if you want – and the meat will be sweet.

- 4 thick, good-quality pork chops
- salt and freshly ground black pepper
- knob of unsalted butter
- 1 apple, unpeeled, cored, and thinly sliced
- 160ml (5½fl oz) cider
- 200ml (7fl oz) chicken stock, plus extra if needed
- 4 tbsp double cream
- 2 tbsp cornflour, whisked with 2 tbsp cold water
- 1 tsp Dijon mustard

Hack

Always buy chops on the bone if you can, as they are less likely to dry out. For the same reason, try to get them at least 2.5cm (1in) thick; thicker is even better!

1. Take the pork chops out of the fridge 1 hour before cooking them, to bring to room temperature.

2. Heat a heavy-based frying pan to the highest possible heat; it needs to be screaming hot, to get a crust on the chops.

3. Dry the pork with kitchen paper and rub salt and pepper all over them, paying extra attention to the fat. Then fry the pork for 2 minutes on each side, turning them with tongs.

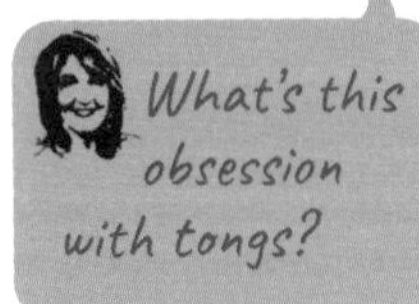

Tongs won't pierce the meat; if you pierce it, all the juices will run out and leave the meat dry

4 Now reduce the heat to medium and cook for another 4 minutes on each side. Remove from the pan and set aside, covered, on a warm plate while you make the sauce.

5 Melt the butter in the same pan in which you fried the pork and fry the apple for a couple of minutes until softened. Remove from the pan with a slotted spoon and set aside on kitchen paper.

6 Still using the same pan (don't clean it, the juices are vital!), place over a medium heat, pour in the cider and let it simmer as you scrape up the crispy brown bits on the pan. Cook for 1–2 minutes, or until the cider has reduced by half.

What does "reduced by half" mean?

Boiled down until there is only half the amount of liquid left in the pan

Continued >>

7 Pour in the stock, bring to the boil, then boil until it, too, has reduced by half.

8 Reduce the heat, add the cream and mustard, and stir gently. Stir in the cornflour mixture and simmer for 20 seconds, stirring. If the sauce is too thick, just add a little more stock.

9 Serve the chops with the apple on top and the sauce drizzled over. (This isn't supposed to be a thick gravy, but a light sauce.) Buttery Carrots with Parsley (see p122) are good with this, as is mustard (if you like), and mashed potato.

FAFF ALERT
It's good to fry some baby onions in butter until golden to add to this, but Kaye probably wouldn't bother.

Kaye most certainly would not - Kaye has already done the washing up and is watching Coronation Street

Banging Bolognese

Serves 4-6

KAYE: This is not so much a recipe, more a faithful servant. I could make it three times a week, swap the pasta for rice or mash, and my kids would never complain. OK, in the interests of full disclosure, I have. The kids never have complained. I use this sauce in lasagne, too. Thank you, my faithful servant.

- 2 tbsp olive oil
- 2 onions, chopped
- 4 garlic cloves, crushed
- 500g (1lb 2oz) minced beef
- 1 tbsp tomato purée or ketchup
- 150ml (5fl oz) dry red wine
- 400ml jar of tomato passata
- 150–200ml (5–7fl oz) beef stock
- salt and freshly ground black pepper
- 2 bay leaves (optional)

Faff alert

I would brown my meat in a dry frying pan, then remove with a slotted spoon before adding the oil and frying the veg, but Kaye finds this very fussy and faffy. I would also add 2 chopped celery sticks and chopped parsley leaves to the onions if I had some lurking in the fridge.

I hate celery

1 Heat the oil in a large heavy-based frying pan over a medium heat.

2 Add the onions and garlic, reduce the heat, and cook for 5 minutes, or until the vegetables have softened.

3 Increase the heat a little, then add the beef and stir until browned.

Use the spoon to break up any clumps of meat

4 Add the tomato purée or ketchup and stir for about 30 seconds.

5 Pour in the wine and bring up to the bubble, stirring the whole time.

6 Pour in the passata and stock, and add ½ tsp salt.

Use a measuring spoon

7 Tuck in the bay leaves (if using), cover, and reduce the heat to a low simmer for 30 minutes to 1 hour, stirring from time to time. Use a heat diffuser if you have one (see p13).

Check every now and again to see if it's drying out – it might need another 50ml (1¾fl oz) or more water added

Swedish-style Meatballs

Serves 4-6

NADIA: I can't call these meatballs what I'd like to call them… but you know that really big furniture shop where you always get so frustrated because it takes hours to go round, and where everything is called blimtong, or nangog, or flipnob? Well, these are a bit like the meatballs you can buy there.

For the meatballs

- 2 tbsp plain flour
- salt and freshly ground white pepper
- 300g (10oz) minced beef
- 300g (10oz) minced pork (this adds moisture to the mix)
- 1 tsp ground allspice
- 2 tbsp fresh breadcrumbs
- 2 tbsp milk
- 1 tbsp vegetable oil
- 1 tbsp unsalted butter

For the sauce

- 1 tbsp unsalted butter
- 1 tbsp plain flour
- 225ml (7½fl oz) beef stock
- ½ tsp soy sauce
- 120ml (4fl oz) double cream

That reminds me; I am right out of lingonberry jam, silly me

1 Put the flour on a dinner plate and season with salt and white pepper.

2 Tip both types of meat, the allspice, breadcrumbs and milk into a bowl, then season well with the salt and pepper and mix well with your hands.

3 Wet your hands (this stops the meat from sticking to them) and roll the mixture into meatballs. You should get 25–30. Toss them in the seasoned flour.

4 Heat the oil in a large, wide pan over a low heat, then add the butter; the butter will bubble. Once the bubbles subside, drop in the meatballs and fry them slowly for 5–8 minutes, turning to cook them on all sides, until golden and cooked through. Using a slotted spoon, remove them from the pan.

You must add the liquid gradually and stir constantly, or the sauce will be lumpy

5 Now make the sauce. Melt the butter in the same pan in which you cooked the meatballs, over a medium-low heat, then add the flour and whisk until golden brown. Still whisking, pour in the stock and let it bubble, stirring until the sauce has thickened. Add the soy sauce and cream. Taste and adjust the seasoning if necessary. Return the meatballs to the pan to reheat.

6 Serve with boiled potatoes, chips, rice, mash, carrots, and lingonberry or cherry jam.

Sesame Stir-fried Beef

Serves 4

NADIA: This recipe was pleaded for by Kaye's youngest girl Bonnie (she's hilarious) because she says Kaye's beef normally has the texture of the sole of her shoe. This one's for you, Bonnie!

Breaking news – I've been awarded Bonnie's greatest accolade: "It's better than Nadia's"

- 450g (1lb) sirloin steak, trimmed of fat
- 4 tbsp light soy sauce
- 1 tsp caster sugar
- 1 tbsp sesame oil
- 2 tsp rice wine or dry sherry
- 4 spring onions, finely chopped
- 2 garlic cloves, crushed
- 2 tbsp vegetable, groundnut, or coconut oil
- large handful of carrot batons
- pre-cooked noodles, to serve

1 Cut the steak into 1cm- (½in-) thick slices against the grain. Meat cut this way is more tender.

You will see which way the fibres run down the meat; you need to cut across those

Apparently it's best if you don't wear rings for this

2 Put the soy sauce, sugar, sesame oil, and rice wine or sherry into a bowl, then add the steak. Now, using your hands, massage the marinade well into the steak.

3 Now add the spring onions and garlic, and stir well.

Just use an ordinary metal spoon, as wooden ones will absorb some of the marinade

Sorry, I don't do marinades, why are you supposed to?

Because it lets the flavours permeate right into each piece of meat and tenderizes it, too

4 Leave this to marinade for 24 hours... or 2 minutes, if that's all you have.

Continued >>

I didn't heat the wok before adding the oil – as you can see, that made Nadia angry

5 Heat up a large frying pan or wok over a high heat, then add the oil. When it's smoking hot, throw in half the beef and stir for 3–4 minutes, or until browned outside and pink in the middle. Put onto a warmed plate.

Don't overcrowd the pan or the meat will steam

6 Repeat with the second batch of meat, adding the carrots to stir-fry at the same time. Meanwhile, reheat the noodles according to the packet instructions. Serve the beef with the noodles.

Faff alert

There's a marinade here. If you want to leave the meat to marinate for a while, plan 24 hours ahead. If you don't, don't.

Something Fishy

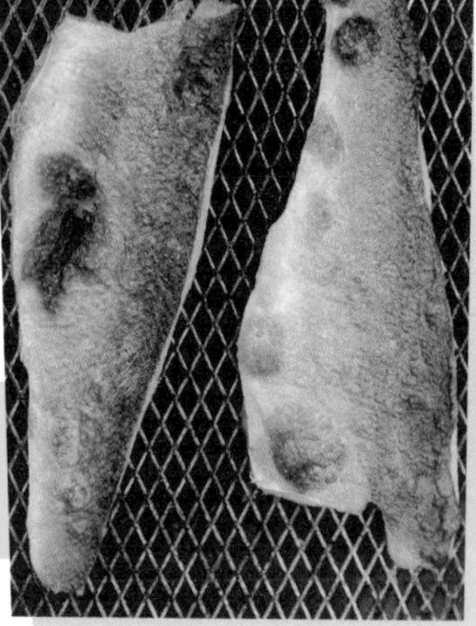

Fail-proof Fish Fillets

Serves 4

NADIA: I call these "fail-proof" because Kaye can cook them perfectly. She makes them at least once a week now, as she adores sea bass. You may wonder if this recipe is cheekily easy but, honestly, it's the simple things that, once perfected, will serve you for a lifetime.

4–8 fillets of white fish
good squeeze of lemon juice
olive oil
sea salt flakes

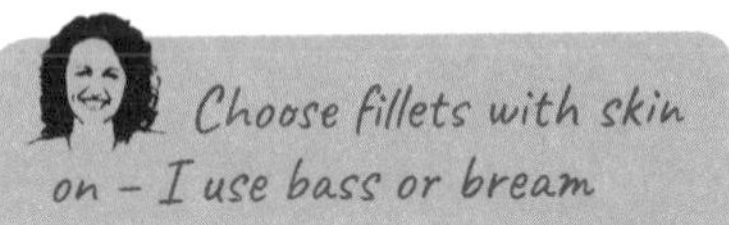

If you can't be bothered to cook them, wear them

1 Start by heating up your grill to the very hottest it can get.

2 Squeeze lemon juice over the flesh side of the fillets, then drizzle them with a little olive oil. Season well with salt.

You don't need to use too much oil here, so be sparing

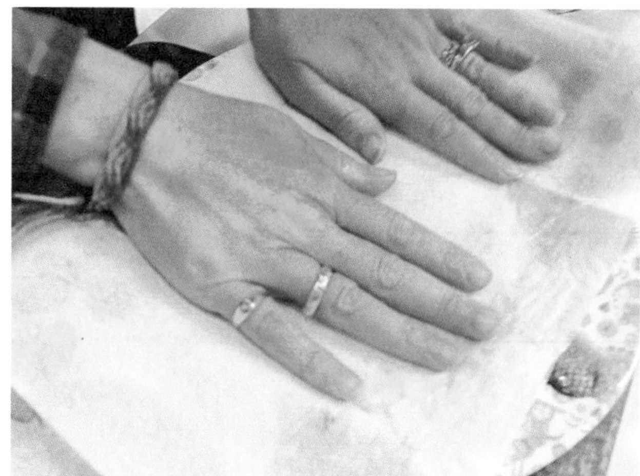

3 Turn the fillets over. Dry the skin thoroughly with kitchen paper, then brush it lightly with olive oil and sprinkle it with more salt. Oil the grill pan, too.

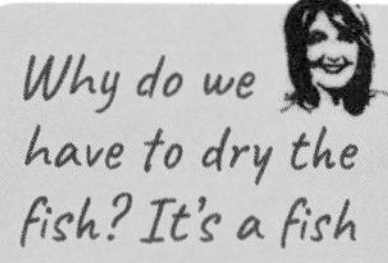

Continued >>

4 Place the fish onto the grill pan, flesh-side down.

5 Put the fish under the grill, as close to the heat as you can get it. Cook for 5–7 minutes.

6 You'll know the fish is ready when the skin has blistered in places and taken on a lovely golden colour.

7 You do not (I repeat *not*) need to turn the fish over and cook on the other side. It will be cooked perfectly as it is.

Nadia told me to use all five senses to tell when they were ready. Could she name the five senses? Could she heck.

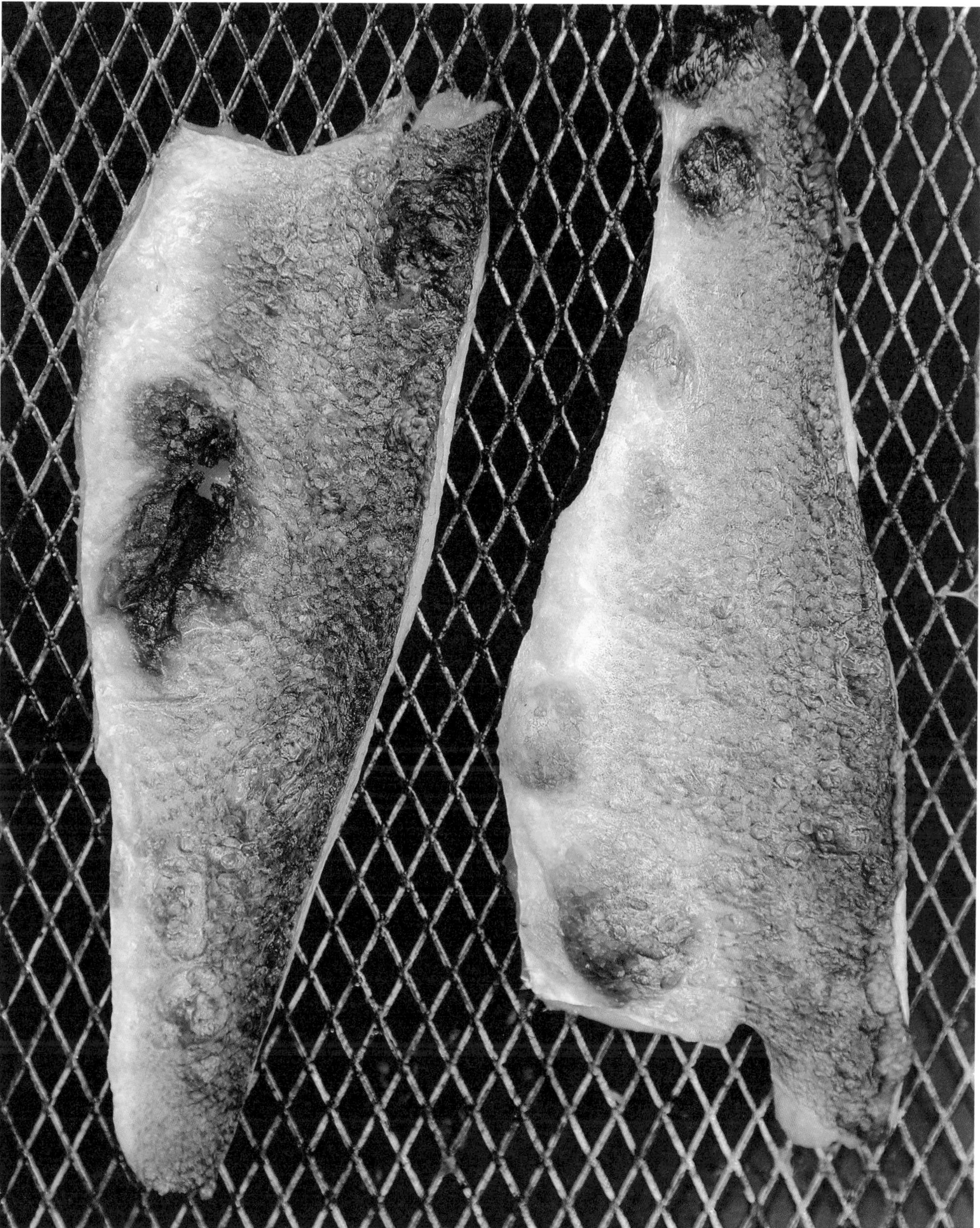

Smoked Haddock & Corn Chowder

Serves 4–6

NADIA: This is a proper meal, rather than just a wishy-washy soup, with lots of big chunks of lovely smoked fish. Try to buy naturally smoked fish, not the fluorescent yellow stuff. Leave the bacon out for pescatarians like Kaye.

- 1 tbsp olive oil
- 8 rashers of smoked streaky bacon, cut into lardons (optional)
- knob of unsalted butter
- 3 leeks, washed and chopped
- 326g can sweetcorn
- 2–3 unpeeled potatoes, scrubbed and chopped
- 600ml (1 pint) whole milk
- 200ml (7fl oz) hot fish stock
- 500g (1lb 2oz) skinless smoked haddock fillet, cut into 4cm (1½in) chunks

1 Heat the oil in a heavy-based large saucepan over a medium heat and fry the bacon (if using) until lovely and brown. Set aside.

Potatoes with skins on? I am liking this already, plus it sounds like a variation on one of my Scottish favourites - cullen skink.

2 Add the butter to the pan, throw in the leeks, and reduce the heat.

3 Cook slowly for 8–10 minutes until softened but not browned. Remove 1 tbsp of the leeks from the pan and set aside. Tip in the sweetcorn.

Don't leave the kitchen; the leeks will need a stir now and again

4 Return half the bacon (if using) to the pan and add the potatoes. Pour in half the milk and all the stock. Bring to the boil.

5 Reduce the heat to a simmer, cover, and cook for 8–12 minutes, or until the potatoes are cooked but not falling apart.

6 Meanwhile, cook the haddock in the remaining milk in another pan – preferably a sauté pan or a deep frying pan – by bringing it up to a gentle simmer for 5 minutes.

It will be opaque all the way through

Continued >>

7 When the fish is cooked, remove with a slotted spoon and keep warm. Pour the haddock milk into the saucepan with the potatoes in, and heat through for just a minute or so for the flavours to blend.

8 Remove half the chowder and blitz in a food processor until smooth.

Only half-fill the food processor and hold a tea towel over the funnel: hot soup burns!

9 Return the puréed chowder to the pan with the rest of the mixture and put it back over a very gentle heat, stirring very gently from time to time until warmed through.

10 Flake in the haddock, keeping the pieces on the chunky side. Serve in warmed bowls with the reserved leeks and lardons (if using) sprinkled on top.

This is quick enough to leave plenty of time for the important things in life.

Tuna & Guacamole

Serves 4

KAYE: I would travel the world in search of the perfect tuna steak. It's my most favourite food ever. And the fancy guac is worth doing even if I can never, *ever* find fresh coriander when I need it. I think an alert goes out to the shops in my area to take it off the shelves just for a laugh.

For the fancy guac

1 large avocado, nice and soft but not bruised

finely grated zest of 1 lime, plus juice of ½ lime, or to taste

¼ small red onion, finely chopped

1 red chilli (deseeded if you don't like it hot), finely chopped

good pinch of sea salt

handful of coriander or parsley, finely chopped

½ small ripe tomato, chopped

For the fish

4 x 150g (5½oz) tuna steaks

drizzle of extra virgin olive oil

1 lemon, cut into 4 wedges

Hack

If not serving straight away, sit the avocado stone in the guacamole, cover with cling film, and pop in the fridge (this will stop the guac turning brown).

1 Halve and peel the avocado, remove the stone, put the flesh in a bowl, and mash roughly with a fork.

2 Add the lime zest and juice, and give it a good stir, then add the onion, chilli, salt, and the coriander or parsley. Mix well, then stir in the tomato. Set aside.

3 Heat a griddle pan over a medium heat, or even over the barbie if you've got that on.

4 Drizzle the tuna steaks with the olive oil and rub salt into them.

5 Wait until the griddle pan is nice and hot (you should be able to see a heat haze, or even smoke, rising from it), then put your tuna steaks in and allow them to sizzle for 2 minutes.

6 Using a fish slice, gently turn over the tuna and cook for another 2 minutes, for medium-rare. (Cook for a minute or so more if you like, but tuna dries out if you overcook it.)

7 Put on a warmed plate and top with a dollop of the guacamole. Serve with lemon wedges. Sliced tomatoes and a little basil, or a green salad, and chips or noodles, are rather fabulous alongside.

I wonder if anyone has invented a pan that tells you when it's at the right temperature – I'd buy it

Pretend Paella

Serves 4

KAYE: I wanted Nadia to devise me a recipe for something *like* a paella, but not a paella, because that would be far too much faff. There's still a lot of chopping in this, but that's what 10-year-olds are for. We wouldn't want a new generation of Disaster Chefs, would we?

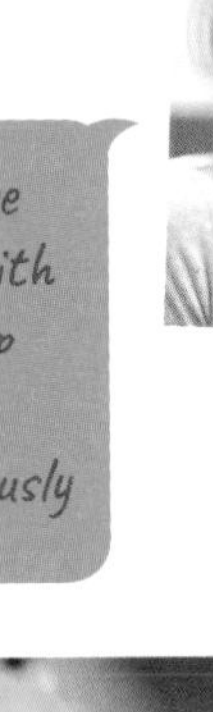

- 2–3 tbsp olive oil
- 2 onions, sliced
- 3 medium tomatoes, cut into 8
- 3–6 garlic cloves, finely chopped
- 300g (10oz) basmati rice
- pinch of saffron threads
- 1 heaped tsp smoked paprika (optional)
- 150ml (5fl oz) dry sherry or white wine
- 400ml (14fl oz) hot fish stock (from a cube is fine)
- 400g pack of frozen seafood mix
- 100g (3½oz) frozen peas
- lemon wedges, to serve
- handful of chopped parsley leaves, to serve

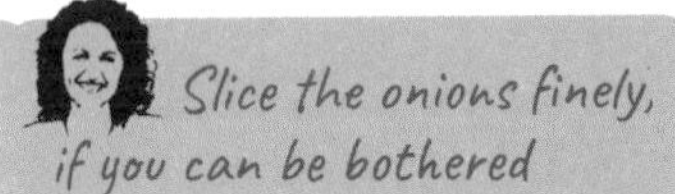

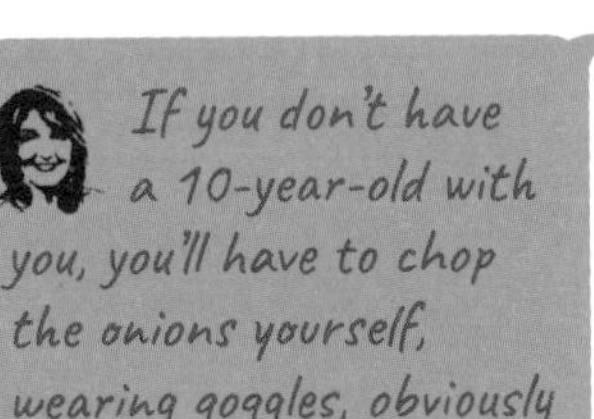

1 Heat the oil in a large frying pan over a medium heat.

2 Add the onions and garlic, and cook for 2–3 minutes, stirring, until softened.

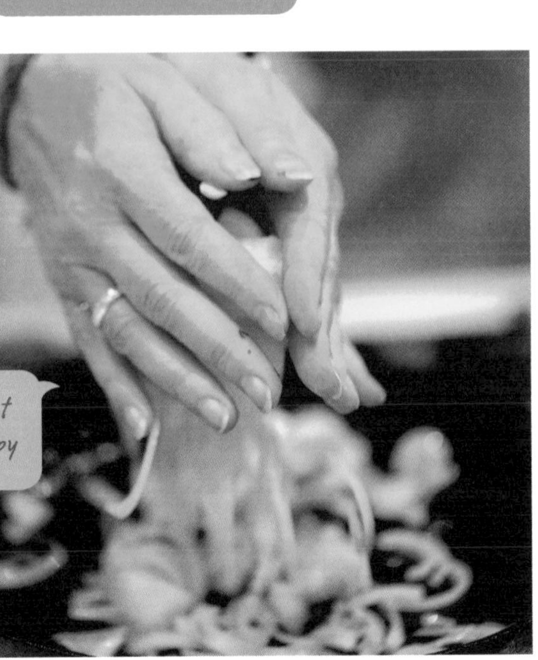

If you can use sherry and smoked paprika, your paella will taste like the real thing

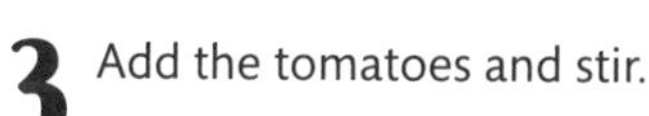

3 Add the tomatoes and stir.

4 Add the rice, saffron, and paprika (if using), and stir for 1 minute.

You can use paella rice in this recipe instead, but basmati rice is quicker to cook

Continued >>

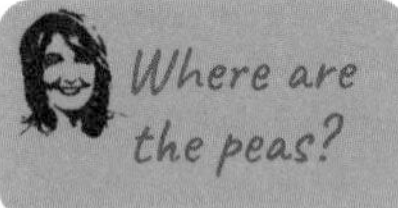

Where are the peas?

Yes, I forgot to add the peas for the photo, but it was still yummy

5 Pour in the sherry or wine. Increase the heat to bring up to the bubble for 1 minute, stirring to burn off the alcohol, then reduce the heat to medium.

6 Add the stock and seafood mix, cover, and simmer very gently for 15 minutes over a low heat, or until the rice and fish are cooked. Add the peas 3 minutes before the end. Don't stir.

7 When the rice is tender and the liquid is absorbed, you're ready to go, with a good squeeze from the lemon wedges, and a flourish of chopped parsley.

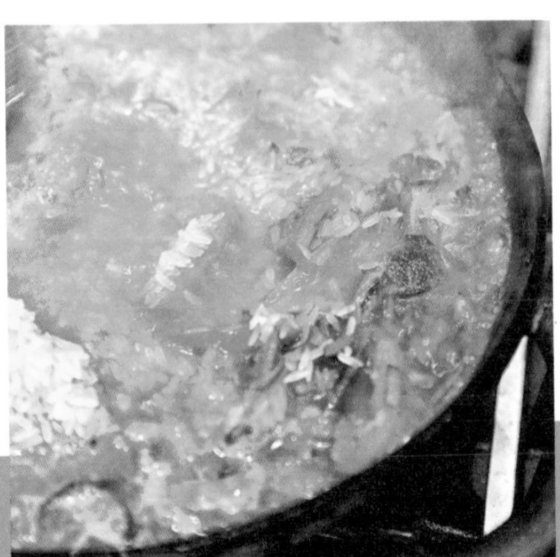

How can you tell when the rice is tender?

Eat some of it!

Feel free to add chunks of fried chorizo, if you eat meat.

Soy Salmon with Egg-fried Rice

Serves 4

KAYE: As a Disaster Chef, making sure the rice is cold before trying to stir-fry it has been a revelation to me. I used to buy pre-packed egg fried rice because mine always looked like pebbledash, but this is the answer.

For the salmon

- thumb-sized piece of fresh root ginger, peeled
- 1 garlic clove, crushed
- 2 tbsp runny honey
- 6 tbsp soy sauce
- 4 salmon fillets, skin on

For the rice

- 2 large eggs, lightly beaten
- ½ tsp salt
- 2 tbsp groundnut or vegetable oil
- 400–600g (14oz–1lb 5oz) cold, cooked rice
- 2 tbsp spring onions, finely chopped

If you haven't got pre-cooked rice, make some (see p17) and lay it on a baking tray until cold

1. Preheat the oven to 180°C (350°F/Gas 4).
2. Grate or finely chop the ginger into a bowl. Mix in the garlic, honey, and soy sauce.

The rule of thumb is to cook fish for 4–6 minutes for every 1cm (½in) of thickness

Oh wait a minute! Let me get a ruler to measure my salmon... nobody ever said

3 Dry the salmon with kitchen paper, then pour the soy marinade over it.

4 Leave to marinate for up to 30 minutes if you've got time; unless it's very hot, the salmon won't need to go in the fridge. After marinating, put the fillets in an ovenproof dish, smoothing the rest of the marinade on top. Cover with foil.

5 Cook in the oven for 12–15 minutes, taking the foil off after 8 minutes.

The honey burns, but the fish is fine

Why has it gone black, oh amazing cook?

Continued >>

6 Meanwhile, make the rice. Mix the eggs and salt in a small bowl and set aside.

7 Heat a wok or large frying pan over a high heat until screaming hot. Pour in the oil.

Stir-frying sets off my smoke alarm

8 When it's smoking hot (watch the smoke alarm!), carefully add the rice and stir-fry for 3–4 minutes, or until thoroughly warmed through.

This is very important – cooked rice, if not reheated properly, can kill you

9 Pour the egg all over the rice and continue to stir-fry briskly for a couple of minutes.

How do I know when the rice is cooked enough?

The eggs should look completely cooked, like omelette

10 Add the spring onions and stir-fry briskly for another couple of minutes. Serve straight away with the salmon.

FAFF ALERT

I like to fry the salmon skin-side down before baking it, to make the skin even crispier, but Kaye would hate to.

Something Veggie

Cheesy Bread & Butter Pud

Serves 4 as a light lunch

KAYE: I don't think I need to explain anything about this recipe except to say, in my best Nigella voice: "Bread, butter, cheese… what could be more perfect?" It will be a surprise to no one that Nadia came up with this on a morning after the night before. Boy, did she feel better afterwards!

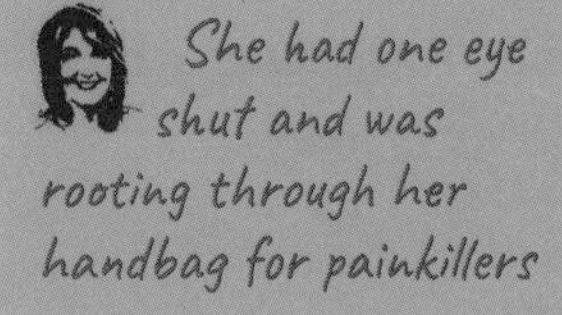

8 slices of generously buttered bread

200g (7oz) of your favourite cheese, grated

For the custard

570ml (1 pint) whole milk

3 eggs, lightly beaten

100g (3½oz) mature Cheddar cheese, grated

4 tbsp grated Parmesan cheese

bunch of chives, chopped

8–10 cherry tomatoes, halved

1 Make 4 sandwiches filled with cheese and cut each into 4 triangle-shaped quarters.

2 Arrange them all in a baking dish, with the pointy bits standing up.

3 Now make the custard. Put the milk, eggs, cheeses, and chives in a jug, give it a good stir, then pour it over the sandwiches. Allow to sit for 30 minutes for the bread to absorb the custard.

4 Meanwhile, preheat the oven to 200°C (400°F/Gas 6). Pop the dish in the oven and cook for 30 minutes, or until the pud is lightly golden.

5 Sprinkle with the cherry tomatoes and serve with a large green salad.

Hack

If you're not veggie, why not add some crispy bacon? Nestle it in under the bread, though, otherwise it might burn in the oven.

Courgetti Spaghetti

Serves 4

NADIA: Kaye begged me to use halloumi as often as I could in this book, as she is slightly obsessed with the stuff. Is it the squeak or the salt, I wonder? Not just halloumi, this dish incorporates every one of her comfort foods. Pasta, avocado, *and* squeaky cheese. Food heaven. You will need a spiralizer (see p13).

- 300g (10oz) dried spaghetti
- 3 courgettes
- 2 tbsp tahini
- 1 large avocado
- 2 tbsp lemon juice, plus extra if needed
- 3–4 tbsp pesto
- salt
- 1–2 tbsp olive oil
- 2 x 250g packs halloumi cheese, sliced 1cm (½in) thick and dried with kitchen paper
- finely grated zest of 1 unwaxed lemon
- handful of basil leaves (optional)

Faff alert

If you like, you can finish this off with a chopped avocado and 1 tsp each black and white sesame seeds, as we did for the photo at the top of the page.

1 Cook the spaghetti according to the packet instructions.

2 Meanwhile, top and tail the courgettes and pass them through a spiralizer. Set aside.

Spiralizing: deeply satisfying and cheaper than therapy

3 Put the tahini, avocado, lemon juice, and pesto into a mini food processor, add 2 tbsp warm water, and blitz. Add a good pinch of salt, then taste and add a little more lemon juice if needed. Set aside.

Don't overcrowd the pan, or the halloumi will steam rather than fry

4 Heat the oil in a large frying pan. Once it's hot, add the halloumi slices (you might need to do this in 2 batches). Cook for 1–2 minutes on each side, until lightly golden. Remove from the pan and put on kitchen paper to blot off excess oil, while you cook the rest. You can also brush the halloumi slices with oil and cook them on a ridged griddle pan, if you prefer, to get those good stripey grill marks. Set aside.

Continued >>

If you want to leave the pasta for the kids and be carb-free, double the amount of courgettes

5 When the pasta is ready, put the spiralized courgettes into a colander. Drain the pasta over the courgettes and stir, to wilt the courgettes. Put both in the dry pasta pan.

6 Stir in the avocado paste and lemon zest, adding a little warm water if it's too sticky.

7 Serve in 4 bowls with the halloumi slices on top. Sprinkle with basil leaves (if using).

Don't mistake tahini for tamari – I did that once: BIG mistake

FAFF ALERT

If you have them in and can be bothered, some toasted pine nuts or sesame seeds go very nicely on top of this!

Moroccan Spiced Chickpeas

Serves 4–6

NADIA: I'm going to be really honest here: I put kale in the recipe to try to be cool, but in fact I hate kale, so would use spinach instead. On another note, you should always put cumin in any recipe containing chickpeas, as it means you will be less farty afterwards!

Canned pulses always need to be drained and rinsed, Lord knows what they can them in, but it's revolting

- 2 tbsp olive oil
- 2 onions, chopped
- 3 garlic cloves, roughly chopped
- 1 heaped tsp baharat spice
- 1 heaped tsp ground cumin
- salt and freshly ground black pepper
- 2 tbsp tomato purée
- 2 tomatoes, roughly chopped
- 300ml (10fl oz) chicken or vegetable stock
- 400g can chickpeas, drained and rinsed
- 250g bag of kale, coarse stalks removed and leaves shredded

And in my spice cupboard: a dear friend gave it to me

1 Heat the oil in a large, heavy-based saucepan over a medium heat. Add the onions and garlic, and cook until softened but not browned.

2 Now add the baharat, cumin, and pepper and fry for 1 minute, stirring. Squeeze in the tomato purée and fry for 30 seconds, then stir in the tomatoes. Pour in the stock, then add the chickpeas.

3 Give it all a good stir, add 100ml (3½fl oz) water, then cover and cook for 15 minutes. Put the kale on top, cover again, and cook for 5–10 minutes until the kale is wilted. Perfect.

Mushrooms & Greens Noodles

Serves 2 as a main or 4 as a side

KAYE: I usually make this recipe for myself. It's one of my favourite veggie dinners, and very quick and easy to make while I am also cooking something meaty for everyone else. If I make double portions, I'll have it cold for my lunch the next day. When we made this for the photos, my dog ate it, so we had to do it again.

- 4–6 spring onions, cut on the diagonal or as you like
- 500g (1lb 2oz) button mushrooms, sliced
- 500g (1lb 2oz) pre-cooked egg noodles
- 1–2 tbsp coconut or vegetable oil
- 2–4 garlic cloves, sliced or crushed (optional)
- 8–10 Tenderstem broccoli spears
- 1 tbsp soy sauce
- 4 tbsp teriyaki sauce
- ½ tbsp dry sherry
- 2 tbsp peanuts (optional)

1 With this or any stir-fry recipe, it really helps to do all the chopping first, so prepare the spring onions and mushrooms and park them next to you by the hob.

Why does the wok have to be hot before you add the oil?

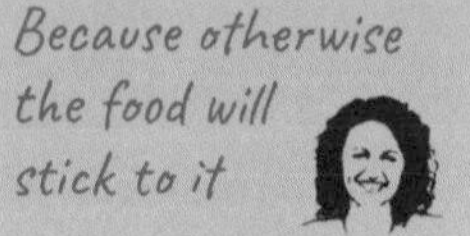

Because otherwise the food will stick to it

2 Heat the noodles in the microwave, according to the packet directions. Then heat a large wok or frying pan over a high heat and pour in the oil.

I had to crush a real garlic clove: Nadia hid my squeezy garlic tube

3 Throw in the spring onions and garlic (if using) and stir briskly for 30 seconds. Throw in the mushrooms, stirring briskly for 2 minutes. Add the broccoli and 1 tbsp water, and continue to stir over a medium-high heat until the broccoli is tender.

Continued >>

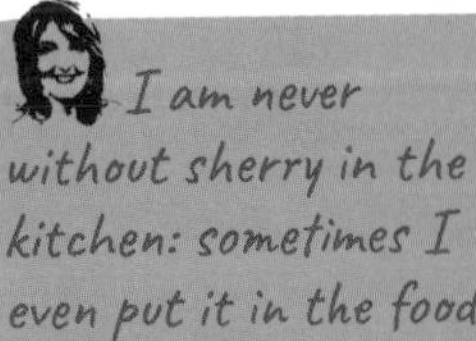

I am never without sherry in the kitchen: sometimes I even put it in the food

4 Add the soy and teriyaki sauces, splash in the sherry, then drop in the hot noodles and stir until they are well mixed in.

5 Sprinkle the peanuts on top (if using) and serve.

Something Slow

KAYE: I really had to stamp my feet to get Nadia to include a slow-cooker section. She just doesn't get the point of them at all. Her idea of heaven is spending two hours a night in the kitchen adjusting the seasoning on her meatloaf. The thought of that makes me want to keel over.

I only discovered slow cookers myself a few months back. A friend suggested it might help me with the "car crash hours" between five and seven in the evening, when you are just in from work and feeling frazzled, with a small pack of hungry animals (children) demanding food. He was right!

It makes my life so much easier. I can potter about when the house has settled down and get all the ingredients for the next day's meal together as I am watching the ten o'clock news. I set the slow cooker on its timer and, the next evening, get home to a ready-to-serve meal. No risk of burning anything, no need to watch over it, and no arguments about what to have. It's done, it's there, it's ready to eat.

I have to be careful not to overdo it, though. My tender lamb got rave reviews the first 100 times, and then they started demanding something that actually requires teeth.

Thai Coconut Red Veg & Beans

Serves 4

KAYE: This is definitely a recipe for a vegetarian. Nadia would need a chicken leg with it. And that's the beauty of it: it's the perfect dish for a mixed family of veggies and meat-eaters. Have it ready for when you get home and, if you want to throw a bit of animal on the plate, feel free.

- 3 tbsp Thai red curry paste
- 225ml (7½fl oz) full-fat coconut milk
- 6 tbsp smooth or crunchy peanut butter
- 1 tbsp soy sauce
- ½ tsp sugar
- 400ml (14fl oz) vegetable or chicken stock
- 6 spring onions, chopped
- 1 red pepper, deseeded and sliced
- 2 courgettes, sliced
- 400g can butter beans or chickpeas, drained and rinsed

1. Put the red curry paste, coconut milk, peanut butter, soy sauce, sugar, and stock into a slow cooker and stir it together.
2. Now add the spring onions, pepper, and courgettes, and put the butter beans or chickpeas on top.
3. Cook on the low setting for 6 hours.
4. Serve with jasmine Perfect Rice (see p17) and your fave green veg.

This is just as good with chickpeas if you don't have butter beans

Chickpeas rather than butter beans every time for me

Faff alert

I serve this with finely grated lime zest, chopped coriander leaves, and peanuts. Kaye does not.

Excuse me, I love peanuts... with a gin and tonic

Moroccan Chicken & Olives

Serves 4

NADIA: I'm going to be honest here: I prefer to cook this (and in fact any simmered dish) on the hob, but Kaye insisted that she wanted *another* slow cooker recipe. Well, of course, she got her wish. This book is an ode to you, Disaster Chef.

A lovely chicken dish without having to stand over a hot stove – what's not to like?

Dry chicken alert: thighs and legs only, not breasts!

- 8 plump, bone-in chicken thighs, skinned
- 2 onions, thinly sliced
- 2 garlic cloves, sliced
- 2 tsp each ground cinnamon, cumin, ginger and coriander
- 1 tsp ground turmeric
- 1 cinnamon stick
- 500ml (16fl oz) chicken stock, made with 2 cubes
- 20 good-quality marinated green olives
- 2 preserved lemons, chopped
- 1 small bunch of coriander, chopped

You don't have to use these, but they do give an authentic Moroccan flavour

Hack

I would fry the onions, garlic, and spices in a little olive oil first, then transfer to the pot. Kaye wouldn't.

1 Put the chicken, onions, garlic, and spices into a slow cooker and pour over the stock. Give it all a good stir.

2 Cook on the low setting for 5 hours, stirring halfway through if you can.

3 Stir in the olives, preserved lemons, and coriander for the last 5 minutes. Serve with harissa sauce.

Slow Cooker Dal

Serves 4

KAYE: I love dal but I don't tend to want to start it from scratch after a long day at work. Making it in the slow cooker with the timer set gives it a real richness of flavour, and means you can be sitting at the table within seconds of getting home. Spoon a dollop of Greek yogurt on the top and scoop it up with warm pitta bread – it's like a warm hug from the inside.

- 2 tbsp olive oil
- 2 onions, sliced
- 4 garlic cloves, crushed
- 2 tsp ground ginger
- salt and freshly ground black pepper
- 3 tsp ground cumin
- 2 tsp cumin seeds
- 2 tsp ground coriander
- ½ tbsp ground turmeric
- 300g (10oz) split red lentils
- 700ml (1¼ pints) vegetable stock
- 200ml (7fl oz) tomato passata
- Perfect Rice (see p17), to serve

1 Heat the oil in a large, heavy-based frying pan over a medium heat. Fry the onions, stirring, until deep golden brown. It will take about 10 minutes.

Don't skip this step or try to rush it. If you try to brown onions quickly, they will burn and scorch, which tastes revolting. They need to be cooked fairly slowly so their sugars caramelize, which gives them the colour. This is the colour you want!

Experiment with the spicing – 2 tsp tamarind would be a good addition – and keep spices in the dark, or they lose flavour

2 Add the garlic, ginger, pepper, ground cumin, cumin seeds, ground coriander, and turmeric, and fry over a medium heat, stirring, for 30 seconds, or until the aromas are released.

3 Scrape the spiced onion mixture out of the frying pan and into the slow cooker.

Why do I need to bother doing this if it's all going in the slow cooker? It seems faffy

It is so worth it; the base to any good curry is well-browned onions and it makes a huge difference to the depth of flavour

Continued >>

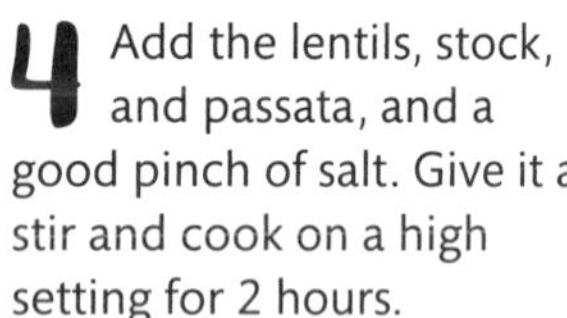

4 Add the lentils, stock, and passata, and a good pinch of salt. Give it a stir and cook on a high setting for 2 hours.

5 Serve with Perfect Rice, or naan, and spinach.

I love loads and loads of fried garlic on top of my dal; I haven't put this in the recipe because Kaye says it's too tiresome to fry garlic separately

It's not that it's too tiresome, but have you ever tried to fry squeezy garlic?

FAFF ALERT

Fry a sliced onion in oil with 1 tsp cumin seeds until golden. Top the dish with this, and a handful of coriander leaves. It makes all the difference.

Garlicky Kleftiko Lamb

Serves 6

NADIA: In winter, I serve this piping hot with piles of rice, and scattered with buttery fried almonds. Then, in summer, when I don't want the oven blazing and can't be bothered to battle with the barbie, I serve the lamb just warm with wraps, Greek salad, and lashings of tzatziki. Mmm. An ice-cold glass of retsina (or two) would be nice, as well!

- **1.5kg (3lb 3oz) shoulder of lamb**
- **lots of salt and freshly ground black pepper**
- **3 tbsp olive oil**
- **1 onion, roughly chopped**
- **4–6 garlic cloves, crushed**
- **1 tsp ground cinnamon**
- **600g (1lb 5oz) potatoes, peeled and cut into cubes**
- **80ml (2¾fl oz) dry white wine**
- **80ml (2¾fl oz) lamb stock**
- **finely grated zest and juice of 1 unwaxed lemon, plus lemon wedges to serve**
- **1 tbsp red wine vinegar**
- **2 tbsp dried oregano**
- **2 tbsp dried thyme**
- **handful of chopped parsley or thyme leaves**
- **handful of black olives**

1 Season the lamb really well with lots of salt and pepper. Make sure your slow cooker is big enough to fit the lamb!

2 Heat the oil in a large frying pan and brown the lamb on all sides. Remove from the pan and set aside.

3 Now put the onion, garlic, and cinnamon in the same pan, season well, and cook over a medium heat, stirring now and again, until softened.

4 Put this onion mixture into the slow cooker, then push the potatoes in, and put the seared (or non-seared, if you didn't bother) lamb on top.

5 Pour the wine, stock, lemon juice, and vinegar over the lamb, then sprinkle in the dried herbs.

6 Cook on the low setting for 9½ hours. If you're around while it is cooking, turn the lamb over once or twice. If you're not, it doesn't matter.

7 The lamb will be falling off the bone – perfect. Sprinkle with the lemon zest, parsley or thyme, and olives and serve with lemon wedges.

This seems a lot of faff – why do I have to brown the meat?

Two reasons: it makes it a good dark colour, and more importantly, it starts to caramelize sugars in the meat, which makes it taste delicious

Dried herbs – now you're talking my language

Beef Bourguignon

Serves 4

KAYE: What a dreamy aroma to come home to: wine, beef… beef, wine… Well, that's what Nadia thinks. Me? I'm more to the point. The dinner is ready. Wine, glass… glass of wine.

- 2 tbsp vegetable oil, plus extra if needed
- 2 tbsp plain flour
- ½ tsp salt and freshly ground black pepper
- 900g (2lb) chuck, braising, or stewing steak, in chunky pieces
- 10 small onions or 1 large onion, sliced
- 4 rashers of streaky bacon, chopped
- handful of button mushrooms
- 2 garlic cloves, crushed
- 2 tbsp tomato purée
- 500ml (16fl oz) dry red wine
- 1 bouquet garni (a bunch of herbs in a muslin bag), or a herby jellied beef stock jelly cube
- pinch of sugar

Good red wine in a beef stew – are you insane?

Not any more than usual – you can taste the wine in this, so, just like any other ingredient, it should be good quality and have a great flavour

1 Heat half the oil in a heavy-based frying pan. Put the flour on a plate and season it very well. Dust the meat in the seasoned flour.

2 Fry half the meat in the pan until browned on all sides, then remove with a slotted spoon, put it in a slow cooker, and repeat for the remaining meat, adding more oil if you need to.

3 Now add the onions or onion slices, bacon, mushrooms, and garlic to the pan, and stir for a few minutes. If you need a little more oil, make sure you heat it up in the pan first. Add the tomato purée and fry for a minute.

4 Pour in the wine, drop in the bouquet garni or stock cube, and bring to the boil, then add the sugar. Pour the contents of the frying pan over the beef.

5 Cook on the low setting for 8 hours. *Do not open for a peek!* If you'd like the sauce thicker, remove the meat with a slotted spoon and boil the sauce until it has reduced (which means some of the excess liquid boils off).

6 Serve with peas and boiled new potatoes. Oh, and garlic bread is nice with this.

Kaye hates doing this, and you could miss it out, but you get more depth of flavour this way

Why do you always make me fry tomato purée?

Because otherwise it can impart a sour taste: frying it makes it sweet

Something Saladу

KAYE: If you are of a similar vintage to me, you might remember what a salad used to look like. I can see it as clear as anything – two leaves of Iceberg lettuce, a block of orange cheese, half a canned peach, a slice of ham, a tomato, and a spoonful of coleslaw. It's little wonder that I always opted for the fish and chips in those days.

We are light years away from that now, with so many different, wonderful ingredients that we can stick in a salad bowl. My problem is that I am not so good on combos and tend to fall back on the same old things, so I was really keen to get some fresh ideas from Nadia on main meal salads. I'd eat them every day if I had more options and, although I love all of the recipes here, I now also feel pretty confident about mixing and matching a bit. The Winter Slaw, especially, is a staple in our house. I can eat it with some leaves and a hunk of freshly baked bread, and I am as happy as a clam, while the rest of the family will have it as an accompaniment to meat or chicken.

The other great thing about salads is that they make me feel better about having a bar of chocolate with my cuppa.

Fruity Halloumi Salad

Serves 4

NADIA: I love this. It is so pretty, fresh, and summery – the kind of dish that is life-affirming to look at! To be honest, I just hack away at the watermelon and get good enough pieces, but you can buy a watermelon slicer that is great for getting chunks and slices out. Not an essential gadget, but useful nonetheless.

For the salad

- a little olive oil
- 250g (9oz) halloumi cheese, cut into cubes, and dried with kitchen paper
- 150g (5½oz) watercress, or green mixed leaf salad
- 10 cherry tomatoes (I used yellow and red), halved if you like
- 500g (1lb 2oz) watermelon, cut into cubes (see recipe introduction)
- 10 raspberries
- 2 tbsp toasted pine nuts (optional, but I would)

For the dressing

- 2 tbsp olive oil
- 1 tbsp lemon juice
- 1 tsp honey or maple syrup
- salt and freshly ground black pepper

1 Heat the oil in a heavy-based frying pan. Add the halloumi cubes and fry for a couple of minutes, until they're a really good golden brown, turning to colour on all sides. Remove the halloumi and place on kitchen paper to blot off excess oil.

2 Scatter the salad leaves on a large plate, add the tomatoes, then the watermelon, and finally, the fried halloumi.

3 Now gently scatter the raspberries and pine nuts (if using) on top.

4 Mix together the dressing ingredients and drizzle over the salad; it should only be lightly dressed.

No, halloumi won't melt as long as the pan is hot, because of its acidity

Winter Slaw

Serves 4–6

KAYE: I tend to make a small bucket of this at a time. There is a bit of chopping involved, so make it worth your while. If I've got some in the fridge, I put it with anything and everything – on the kids' sandwiches, on oatcakes, with my favourite veggie burger, on my eyes to get rid of the bags… you get the picture.

For the slaw

- 1 small, sweet, pointed cabbage
- ½ red cabbage
- 2 small green apples, unpeeled
- 1 tbsp each pumpkin seeds, sesame seeds, and sunflower seeds
- 8–10 walnut halves

For the dressing

- 1 tbsp white wine vinegar, or to taste
- 2 tbsp olive oil, or to taste
- 1 tsp Dijon mustard, or to taste
- salt and freshly ground black pepper

1 Remove the outer leaves of both cabbages so you only have nice crisp inner leaves. Slice as thinly as you can in a food processor, with a mandoline, or by hand with a really sharp knife. Put in a large bowl.

2 Core and finely chop the apples, and add to the cabbage with the seeds. Toss really well so all the ingredients are evenly mixed.

3 Whisk together all the dressing ingredients and taste, then adjust the ingredients as you prefer. Drizzle over the top of the slaw, mixing well until it is lightly coated.

4 Top with the walnuts.

Sharp knives are less likely to slip than blunt knives, so you're actually less likely to cut yourself

Chicken Mango Chilli Salad

Serves 4

KAYE: So good, you forget it's healthy. Even I can't go wrong with this, which might be why I like salads so much. The mango makes it taste really special and a bit of a treat, and I use prawns instead of chicken, which is delicious. I don't want to inflate her ego too much, but Nadia's salad dressing is ace. Make more than you need and keep it in the fridge. It's fine for up to a week.

For the salad

- 4 cooked chicken breasts, skin on
- 1 large ripe mango
- 100g bag mixed salad leaves
- 100g bag watercress
- 3 tbsp pistachio nuts

For the dressing

- 4 tbsp olive oil
- 1½ tbsp white balsamic vinegar or white wine vinegar
- 1 red chilli, finely chopped (and deseeded if you don't like it hot)
- 1 tsp Dijon mustard
- salt and freshly ground black pepper

1 Before you start, take the chicken out of the fridge and allow it to come to room temperature.

If you use it fridge-cold, it will be hard and dry

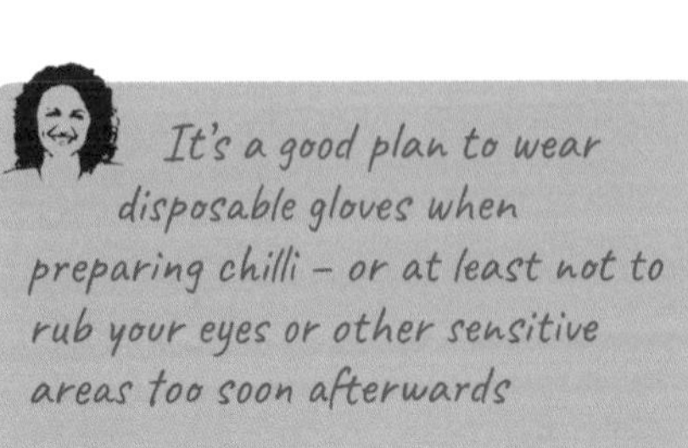

2 To prepare the mango, slice off both "cheeks" on either side of the stone.

How do I know where the stone is?

Look at the mango from the stalk end – the stone runs along the length of this cross-section

3 Now cut a cross-hatch pattern into the flesh of both "cheeks". Push the skin inside out; the cubes of mango will stand up and it will look a bit like a hedgehog. Slice off the cubes. Set aside.

You do know that you can buy it ready-chopped in tubs from the supermarket?

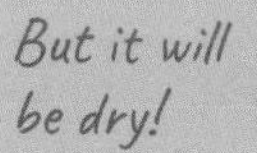

But it will be dry!

Continued >>

4 In a small bowl, mix together all the dressing ingredients.

5 Put the lettuce, watercress, and mango into a separate bowl, drizzle half the dressing over, and toss very well, so everything is lightly coated. Divide between 4 plates.

6 Slice the chicken breasts as neatly as you can and put them on top of the salad. Drizzle the rest of the dressing over the chicken.

Be generous with the dressing, no one wants dry chicken

I am going for lovely juicy prawns here instead of chicken if that's OK, Chef?

7 Sprinkle the pistachios equally between the 4 plates and serve.

EXTRA FAFF

There are lots of additions you could make to this. Try adding avocado chunks. Or even take out the chicken and serve the fruity salad as a side to spicy barbecue food.

Roast Carrot & Aubergine Rice

Serves 2 (or 4 as a side dish)

NADIA: Kaye loves this dish and can now make it really well. I have finally convinced her of the merits of preheating the oven, so she no longer burns every vegetable she tries to roast. By the way, if you're not a vegetarian, this goes really well as a side with lamb.

Preheating the oven works. I've incinerated more aubergines than I care to remember; who wants to be the person who burns the salad?

For the salad

1 aubergine, cut into 2.5cm (1in) cubes

2 carrots, peeled and cut into batons

2–3 tbsp olive oil

sea salt

1 tsp ground cinnamon (optional)

250g bag pre-cooked brown and wild rice

large handful of flat-leaf parsley leaves, chopped

For the dressing

juice and finely grated zest of ½ unwaxed lemon, or to taste

2 tbsp olive oil

salt

1 Preheat the oven to 200°C (400°F/Gas 6).

2 Toss the veg in the oil, salt, and cinnamon (if using), and space out on a baking tray in a single layer. Roast for 30 minutes, turning halfway through.

3 Meanwhile, mix together all the dressing ingredients, whisking with a fork until the oil and lemon emulsify, which means the oil incorporates completely with the other ingredients. Taste, adjust the seasoning, and add more lemon if you like.

Because otherwise they will steam rather than roast, and you won't get those yummy crispy bits

4 Put the rice and parsley in a large bowl with the roasted veg, and pour the dressing over.

5 Stir well and serve!

Don't care what you say, as far as I'm concerned, this serves one – me!

Hack

Choose aubergines that are heavy for their size, with taut, shiny skins. They will have the juiciest and freshest flesh.

Roast Veggies with Garlic Mayo

Serves 4–6

KAYE: If cooking is about trial and error, I have made more mistakes than most, and no more so than with roasted veggies. In my head, it is so simple: cut 'em, oil 'em, and stick 'em in the oven. Unfortunately, that has too often ended in "call the fire brigade". So be warned, stick to the rules: preheat the oven, cut the veggies in equal sizes, and don't pack them three deep.

2 carrots
1 aubergine
1 large courgette
1 green pepper, deseeded
1 red pepper, deseeded
6 whole garlic cloves (optional)
2–3 tbsp olive oil
salt and freshly ground black pepper

For the mayo

10 tbsp mayonnaise
½–1 garlic clove, crushed
2 tsp lemon juice
2 tsp olive oil

1 Preheat the oven to 200°C (400°F/Gas 6).

2 Cut the vegetables into equal-sized pieces. Lay them on 2 baking trays with the garlic (if using), making sure the veggies are not too close together.

3 Drizzle the olive oil over, starting with the aubergine as it will need the most oil. Almost massage the oil into the veg before seasoning well with salt and pepper.

4 Cook for 30 minutes, turning after 15 minutes. (Check for tenderness with a knife.) The veggies should be charred but not burned.

5 Meanwhile, in a small bowl, whisk together the mayonnaise, garlic, lemon juice, and oil. (Be warned: if you use a whole clove of garlic, the mayo will be pretty punchy.) Serve with the roast veggies.

So should I use my biggest baking tray?

Not necessarily, just use your judgement: if the veggies are too spread out, they'll burn

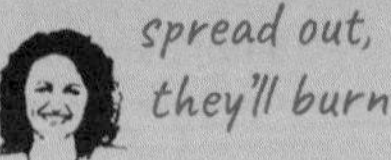

Don't forget this bit, as they may need 10 minutes more, depending on your oven

Hack

If you have some chives or parsley hanging about, chop them up and throw them into the mayo, too.

Something on the Side

KAYE: I was so smug when my eldest daughter was a toddler. She would happily wolf down any and every vegetable you put in front of her, loved hummus, devoured olives. All those hours of mushing up green beans and asparagus had clearly paid off.

Then came along daughter number two. Same mush, different outcome. Her palate was, and still is, more beige than an interior decorator's shade card. I have lost sleep over getting veggies into that girl. If I insist, she will literally hold her nose and shovel them in, making retching sounds as she does it. And that can play havoc with a mother's self-esteem. If I try to hide the veg, she sniffs them out. In despair, I turned to Nadia. "Why, oh why," I asked her, "will Bonnie not eat vegetables?"

The answer was short and not sweet: "Because your vegetables are disgusting." Boiled-to-death broccoli, tasteless carrots, and soggy spinach. I couldn't deny it. Because I don't eat meat, my veggie meals are the main event. When I'm cooking for anyone else, vegetable side dishes tend to be only an afterthought.

Just a teeny bit of extra effort – a dollop of butter and parsley, some cheese, a sprinkling of care and attention – really can make a world of difference.

Broccoli with Mint & Feta

Serves 4-6

KAYE: This is a super-simple, interesting way of serving this veg, and am I glad to discover a way to jazz up my broccoli! One of my daughters in particular is veg-resistant, and this little twist makes all the difference.

For the broccoli

400g (14oz) Tenderstem broccoli
salt
200g (7oz) feta cheese

For the dressing

2 tbsp olive oil
finely grated zest and juice of ½ unwaxed lemon
6–8 mint leaves, finely chopped, or 1 tsp dried mint
za'atar, to serve (optional)

I am not even going to pretend I keep fresh mint in the fridge – dried stuff does the trick

Hack

Steaming broccoli keeps it firm and tasty, and stops the nutrients leaching out into the water, which can happen if you boil it.

1 Season the broccoli with salt and place it in a steamer basket. Steam over a medium-high heat for 4–6 minutes, depending on the size of the spears and how tender you like them, or until the point of a sharp knife can pierce a thick stalk with no resistance.

2 Meanwhile, mix together all the dressing ingredients.

3 Transfer the broccoli to a serving dish. Crumble the feta cheese on top, drizzle with the dressing, toss, and serve, sprinkled with za'atar (if using).

Whole Cauli Cheese

Serves 4–6

KAYE: Well, this is a first. Last time I looked in Nadia's microwave, it still had cardboard packaging in it, along with a can of root concealer for her hair and some spare contact lenses. This is a cool way to make cauliflower cheese and, as a more frequent microwave user, it's right up my street.

Turn the cauli upside down and trim off the base, then remove a cone-shaped piece of the core

1 whole cauliflower, leaves trimmed off
1 quantity Perfect Cheese Sauce (see p16), hot and freshly made
100g (3½oz) grated cheese (whichever cheese you like)

1 Using a small paring knife, remove and discard the innermost portion of the cauliflower core without cutting off the florets. This will help to cook the cauliflower all the way through.

2 Put the cauliflower, cored-side down, in 2.5cm (1in) of water in a microwave-safe dish. Cook in the microwave on high for 7–10 minutes. Drain.

3 Top with the hot cheese sauce and sprinkle with the grated cheese.

You can pop it under a hot grill for extra colour after adding the grated cheese, if you like

Faff alert

I would add some fried onions to the cheese sauce.

Buttery Carrots with Parsley

Serves 4

NADIA: Kaye always bemoans the fact that her children won't eat vegetables, but she usually either overcooks or undercooks them, with not even a flash of butter or olive oil, so it's no wonder her kids run for the hills when she makes them. This is a simple, effective way to tart up a carrot.

Is steaming really that much better than chucking them in a pan of boiling water?

- 6–8 carrots, cut into rounds
- sea salt
- good knob of unsalted butter
- ½ onion, finely chopped or grated
- ½ small bunch of flat-leaf parsley, finely chopped

1 Place the carrots in a steamer basket and sprinkle with salt. Place over steaming water over a medium-high heat for 3–6 minutes, depending on how tender you like your carrots (test with the tip of a knife).

Yes, if you boil them, it's too easy to get waterlogged, soggy carrots

2 When the carrots are cooked, remove the steamer basket from the heat and set aside, still covered.

3 Pour away the water from the steamer base, place it over a low heat, and melt the butter in it. When the butter is just melted, add the onion and stir for 1 minute.

Protect your hands and arms, as steam burns!

4 Return the carrots to the pan, stir them with the onions, then throw in the parsley and serve.

Red Cabbage with Apples

Serves 6

NADIA: Kaye doesn't really have the patience to cook anything long and slow (unless it's in her beloved slow-cooker), so this is a speeded-up version of an old classic. It's excellent on a plate with regular or veggie sausages.

Hmmm... if you say so Nadia, but this is definitely a weekend dish for me; we don't all have the time to loll around the kitchen drinking rosé, you know

- small knob of unsalted butter
- 1 onion, sliced
- 1 red cabbage, cored and shredded
- 2 bay leaves
- 1 tsp ground cinnamon
- 200ml (7fl oz) hot chicken stock
- 50g (1¾oz) soft brown sugar or any sugar you've got
- 75ml (2½fl oz) white wine vinegar or cider vinegar
- 2 apples, peeled, cored, and cut into wedges

1 Melt the butter over a medium heat in a lidded heavy-based saucepan, and fry the onion until it becomes translucent.

2 Add the cabbage, bay leaves, cinnamon, hot stock, sugar, and vinegar, and bring to the boil, then cover and reduce the heat to a low simmer for 30 minutes (use a heat diffuser, see p13).

3 Stir in the apples and cook for another 20 minutes. Remove the bay leaves and serve. This is good with Sticky Sausage & Onion Bake (see p40).

Hack

This is better made the day before you need it, as the flavours mingle and improve overnight. You can also freeze it, then defrost it and reheat in a saucepan when needed.

If you're tempted to put the red cabbage in your document shredder, I can confirm it is not a good idea

Peas with Spring Onion & Salami

Serves 6 (at least)

NADIA: How posh are these peas? And only a teeny bit of extra faff. They are pretty good without the salami, too, if you are a non-meat eater like Kaye. Or you could stir in a dollop of mascarpone for a creamy version.

- 500g (1lb 2oz) petits pois
- large knob of unsalted butter, plus more, to serve (optional)
- 6 spring onions, finely sliced
- 1 garlic clove, finely sliced
- 6 slices of salami, finely chopped
- salt and freshly ground black pepper

Hack

Don't buy garden peas by mistake – yuck! They tend to be mealy and tough. Petits pois are far more tender.

1 Cook the peas in boiling water, according to the packet instructions.

2 Meanwhile, heat the butter in a non-stick saucepan, throw in the spring onions, and cook over a low heat until softened but not browned. Add the garlic for the final minute.

3 When the peas are ready, drain them well, then add them to the spring onion pan and throw in the chopped salami. Season to taste and serve with another knob of butter if you're feeling decadent.

I strongly advise you use a heat diffuser for this recipe *(see p13)*

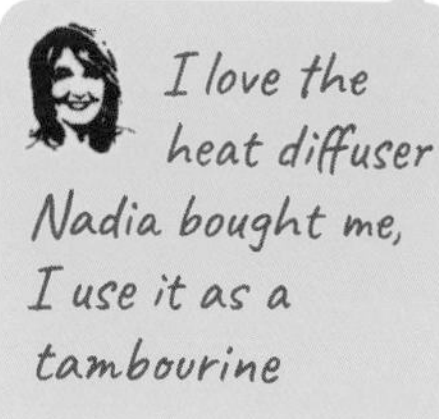

Something for the Weekend

KAYE: All rules go out the window at the weekend. Anything goes. If you fancy a Marshmallow & Bacon Butty washed down by a Healthy-ish Choc Nut Smoothie at 3 o'clock on a Saturday afternoon, just go for it. It's all about having something you fancy.

It's also about having a bit more time than you normally have during the week and, for me, about being able to relax with my kids rather than barking at them to finish their homework.

I don't know where my teenage daughter gets it from, but she's a great baker and she swears by Nadia's Perfect Victoria Sponge recipe, while the little one and I love messing about making my Slapdash Scones.

As a Disaster Chef, I would never normally attempt a full roast dinner but Nadia, bless her, has laid that out in this chapter with military precision. I confess I stuck a post-it note to my forehead with all the timings on the first time I attempted it, but it does get easier. Follow Sergeant Major Sawalha's instructions and you can't go wrong.

Luxury Coconut Bircher

Serves 4

NADIA: There are some quite pricey ingredients in this recipe, the kind that would make Kaye want to go for a lie-down, but it *is* the weekend and it's been a loooong week. Feel free to add nuts or any dried fruits, if you prefer.

It's about time, I've banged on about oats since I met Nadia and she turned up her nose; one week in vegan boot camp and she's a convert

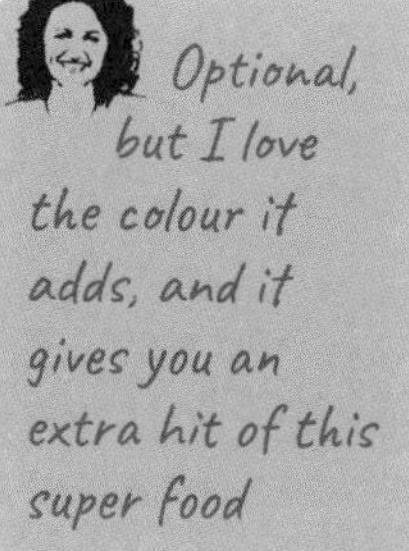

- 150g (5½oz) porridge oats
- 200ml (7fl oz) coconut water or just plain water
- 2 heaped tsp blueberry powder (optional)
- 1 heaped tbsp sunflower seeds
- 6 dried apricots, finely sliced
- 2 tbsp desiccated coconut
- 30g (1oz) blueberries, plus 50g (1¾oz) extra to serve
- 20g (¾oz) raspberries, plus 50g (1¾oz) extra to serve
- 4 tbsp coconut yogurt
- 1 apple, grated
- sesame seeds, to serve

1 Put the oats, coconut water or water, blueberry powder (if using), sunflower seeds, apricots, coconut, and 30g (1oz) blueberries and 20g (¾oz) raspberries into a Tupperware pot.

2 Give it a good stir.

3 Cover and put in the fridge overnight.

4 Spoon into 4 small bowls, stir in the yogurt and apple, and scatter the extra blueberries, raspberries, and sesame seeds on top.

Hack

Add 1 tbsp honey or good-quality maple syrup if you like things a bit sweeter. And you can always add a little milk if you like a looser bircher (that sounds rude, somehow).

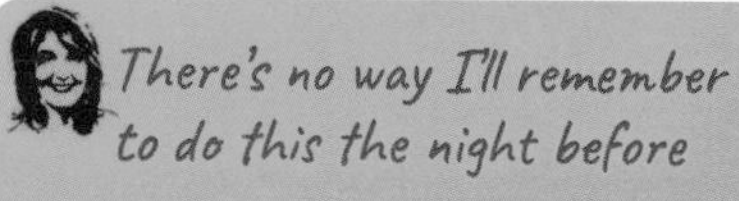

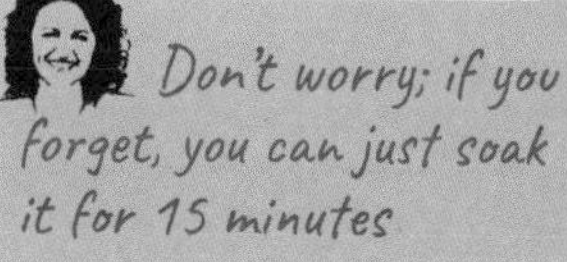

Slapdash Scones

Makes 6-ish

KAYE: I am still a bit gleeful when I think of Nadia's initial reaction to this recipe. It was handwritten on a crumpled piece of paper by a fellow Disaster Chef and friend of mine, and Nadia was convinced it would be an epic fail. Well, she ate her words and at least three of my scones! Liberate yourselves from measuring cups and weighing scales – go freestyle!

For the scones

unsalted butter, chilled
self-raising flour
pinch of salt
1 egg, lightly beaten
whole milk

For the optional extras

grated cheese
caster sugar
sultanas
vanilla extract

1 Preheat the oven to 180°C (350°F/Gas 4).

The book people made me put this step in – it's not on my piece of paper

2 Cut roughly one quarter of a pack of butter into wee blocks.

3 Tip roughly the same amount (by eye) of flour into a large mixing bowl, and add the salt and cubes of butter.

And for those of us who need NUMBERS, this means 225g (8oz) self-raising flour and around 40g (1½oz) butter

4 Rub the butter into the flour with your fingertips until you get a crumb-like mixture.

If you lift your hands high out of the bowl while rubbing with your fingertips, the mixture will become lighter

That's not in my recipe either

5 Add the egg, mix, then splash in a wee drop of milk to make a big, solid dough thing.

6 Now choose your flavouring. I added 40g (1½oz) grated Cheddar cheese to mine, because that's my favourite. Mix well.

Or make them sweet – just add caster sugar, sultanas, vanilla, whatever you fancy!

Which means (for the rest of us): add 40g (1½oz) sugar or 20g (¾oz) sultanas, plus a few drops of vanilla extract

Continued >>

7 Once it's all mixed in, flatten your mixture out to about 2.5cm (1in) thick, then divide the mixture into however many scones you fancy (I like 5 or 6 large ones).

I just fashion my scones freestyle – works for me!

I would push a biscuit cutter or glass straight down into the mixture without twisting – that's how to get your scones to rise

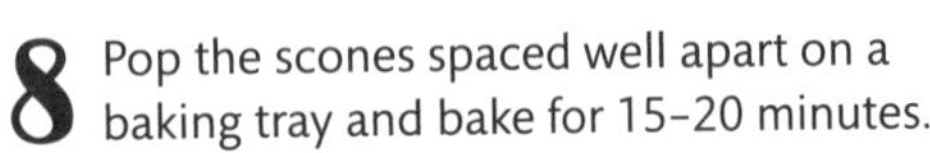

8 Pop the scones spaced well apart on a baking tray and bake for 15–20 minutes.

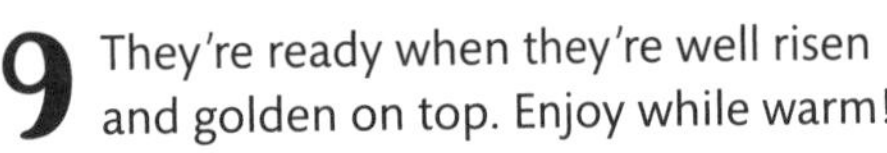

9 They're ready when they're well risen and golden on top. Enjoy while warm!

Perfect Roast Dinner

Serves 4

KAYE: I claim diplomatic immunity. Nobody in Scotland has a sit-down dinner at 2pm on a Sunday. So, I assume this is training for the meal guaranteed to bring a Disaster Chef out in a cold sweat: Christmas dinner. In addition to Nadia's ingredients, I recommend a small jar of smelling salts.

For a lovely full roast dinner, you'll be making Perfect Roast Chicken, Perfect Roast Potatoes, Perfect Yorkshire Puds, Perfect Gravy, and Buttery Carrots with Parsley (see pp138–145 and p122). Take a deep breath: you can do it!

DAY BEFORE

If you can, prepare your Yorkshire batter the night before and leave it in the fridge.

-4 hours

Take the batter out of the fridge if you remember (it rises more if not fridge-cold). Prepare the chicken.

-2¼ hours

Preheat the oven to its highest setting.

-2 hours

Put the chicken in the oven. Prepare the potatoes up to the end of step 3 (see p140). Peel and slice the carrots, and leave them to soak in cold water.

-1½ hours

Whack the roasting tin and oil or fat for the potatoes in the oven. Baste the chicken; add the wine to its tin. Reduce the oven temperature to 200°C (400°F/Gas 6).

-1 hour

Turn the chicken over. Spoon the potatoes into the fat on the top shelf of the oven (it will spit, so watch out). Pour oil into the Yorkshire pud tray and put in the oven.

-35 minutes

Increase the oven temperature again to its highest setting. Remove the chicken from the oven; keep warm.

-30 minutes

Turn the potatoes. Pour the Yorkshire pud batter into the hot fat and bake. Make the gravy; keep it warm.

-15 minutes

Put the kettle on to boil for the peas.

-10 minutes

Put the carrots on to steam.

-5 minutes

Pour boiling water from the kettle into a saucepan and tip in frozen peas. Add the onion butter to the carrots. Remove the potatoes and Yorkshires from the oven.

DINNER TIME

COME AND GET IT!!!!

Perfect Roast Chicken

Serves 4

KAYE: There is nothing quite like the aroma of a chicken roasting for making you feel cosy and loved. I usually buy a bird in a bag and whack it straight in the oven but, hey, why not give it a go the old-fashioned way?

- 4 onions, quartered
- 6 garlic cloves
- 2 carrots, halved lengthwise
- 1.6kg (3lb 5oz) chicken
- 2 tbsp unsalted butter, softened
- 2 tsp dried mixed herbs
- salt and freshly ground black pepper
- 1 glass dry white or dry rosé wine (optional... but go on!)

1 Preheat the oven to its highest setting. Put the onions, garlic, and carrots into a roasting dish.

2 Dry the chicken with a piece of kitchen paper, then rub it all over with the butter, sprinkle with the herbs, and season well.

3 Lay the bird breast-side down in the roasting dish, put it in the oven, and cook for 30 minutes.

4 Pour the wine (if using) around the chicken. Spoon the winey juices over the bird, then reduce the oven temperature to 200°C (400°F/Gas 6).

5 Cook for another 30 minutes, then turn the chicken over, trying not to pierce the skin.

6 Return to the oven and cook for another 20–25 minutes until golden brown. Allow to rest for at least 15 minutes; if you cut into the chicken too early, all the juices will run out rather than stay in the bird and it will be dry.

If you shake the leg and it moves easily, that means it's cooked through

How on earth do you pick up a hot chicken?

I use tongs or stick a wooden spoon up its jacksie

Perfect Roast Potatoes

Serves 4–6

NADIA: Kaye really had a go at me when she read this recipe. "What the hell does parboil mean?" It means partially cook. By boiling. It's a short step from good roasties to oily mess, but follow my tips and all will be well.

I got a bit tearful reading this. My kids have never tasted home-made roast potatoes. Everybody say, "Ahhhhh"

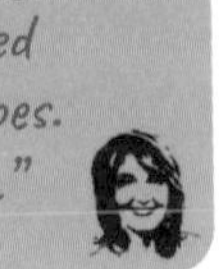

- 4–6 tbsp vegetable oil or duck fat
- 12 potatoes, such as Desirée, Maris Piper, or King Edward
- 1 tsp salt, plus extra to serve
- piece of bread, for testing

1 Preheat the oven to its highest setting. Pour the oil or spoon the fat into a roasting tin and place on the middle shelf.

2 Peel the potatoes and cut into quarters or evenly sized chunks. Put into a large saucepan, add the salt, then pour in cold water to cover. Bring to the boil, then simmer for 12 minutes. Drain.

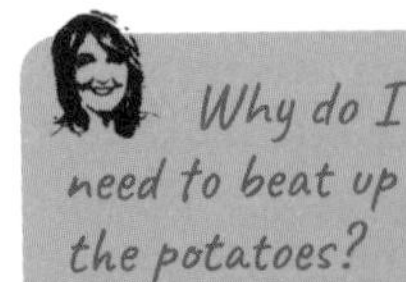

Why do I need to beat up the potatoes?

3 Return the potatoes to the saucepan, cover with the lid and, holding the lid in place, shake the potatoes around to roughen and fluff up their edges.

Because it makes your roasties crisp

4 Remove the roasting tin from the oven and place the piece of bread in the oil. If it begins to sizzle straightaway, remove the bread and add the potatoes in an even layer. If not, return the tin to the oven for another 5 minutes before testing again.

Do not cover to keep them warm, as trapped steam will soften the all-important crispy bits!

5 Once the potatoes are in the oven, reduce the temperature to 200°C (400°F/Gas 6). Roast for 30 minutes.

Don't be tempted to open the oven door, as you'll reduce the temperature and risk soggy roasties

6 Remove the roasting tin from the oven and place on the hob over a medium heat. Carefully turn all the potatoes over, then return the tin to the oven for another 30 minutes, or until the potatoes are golden and crispy.

7 Take them out once they have turned an even golden brown. Carefully remove them using a slotted spoon, sprinkle with salt, and serve immediately.

Perfect Yorkshire Puds

Makes 12

NADIA: I love a great roast dinner. There is nothing about it I don't like: lots of meat, relaxed (hopefully) friends and family, a glass of wine in the middle of the day, and the knowledge that there's a pud to come. But I could honestly do away with everything else and just have Yorkshires and gravy.

I don't think I've ever tasted a Yorkshire pudding. They are just not a Scottish thing. Can you put chocolate in the middle?

Actually, yes, I love 'em with jam or golden syrup, just don't serve those with a roast dinner

12 tsp vegetable oil, beef dripping, or lard
225g (8oz) plain flour
1 tsp salt
4 eggs
300ml (10fl oz) skimmed milk

Hack

If you like your Yorkshires to be slightly denser, with a dent in the middle, make sure your batter is cold before you pour it into the tray.

1 Preheat the oven to its highest setting. Put 1 tsp oil, dripping, or lard in each hole of a 12-hole muffin tray, and put the tray in the oven.

2 Meanwhile, put the flour and salt in a large bowl and make a well (this means a big hole) in the middle.

3 Put the eggs and milk in a jug and mix gently, then pour into the well, whisking to mix the flour in from the sides until you have a smooth batter.

4 Pour the batter back into the jug and leave to rest for a minimum of 15 minutes.

5 Wait until the fat in the muffin tray is smoking hot. This is very important because, if the oil isn't hot enough, the Yorkshires won't rise. Pull the baking tray halfway out of the oven and very quickly divide the batter equally between the muffin holes.

6 Close the oven door and cook for 20–25 minutes, or until well risen and golden. Serve immediately with lashings of gravy.

Even better, prepare the batter the night before; the Yorkshires will rise much higher, but I usually only manage 15 minutes

Perfect Gravy

Serves 6–8

NADIA: Gravy is something that so many people worry about. It's too easy to give up and buy a tub of gravy granules. Please, we implore you, don't do that. It's revolting. Really, it is. And, we promise, just follow these instructions and your home-made gravy will be divine.

I don't worry about gravy. I never gave it a thought before this; I just dissolved a cube in water. Now I can see that gravy is a 'thing'

- cooking juices from a roast
- up to 1 litre (1¾ pints) chicken stock

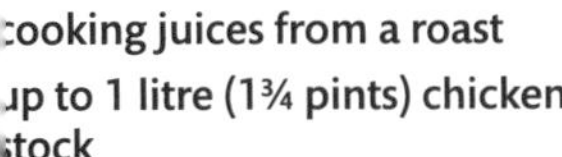

- 1 tbsp plain flour
- 120ml (4fl oz) dry white wine (or it's OK to use dry red wine or dry sherry)

Go gradually, adding a little at a time, to avoid lumps

Hack

If the gravy turns out lumpy, just press it through a sieve with the back of a spoon.

1 Lift the roast out of the roasting tin without piercing the skin (I do this with a chicken by sticking a wooden spoon into the cavity and letting all the juices from the insides pour into the tin).

2 Tilt the roasting tin and spoon off most of the fat from the surface of the juices, reserving 1 tbsp.

3 Remove any veg and garlic you used from the tin with a slotted spoon and blitz them in a blender until smooth. Pour into a measuring jug and top up to 1 litre (1¾ pints) with stock.

4 Place the roasting tin over a medium heat with the reserved fat, and scrape up the yummy bits from the base.

5 Then sprinkle in the flour and, using a whisk, whisk briskly over a medium heat.

6 Now, still whisking, pour in the wine or sherry, and cook for 30 seconds, still over a medium heat.

7 Finally, pour in the blended veg and stock mixture, and keep whisking until the gravy is nicely blended, smooth, and thickened. Keep warm until ready to serve.

Cinnamon Berry Mug Cake

Serves 1

KAYE: It's not for me, this one, to be honest. If I am that desperate for sugar, I'll go chocolate every time, but the kids just love making these. So, in the interests of half an hour's peace, it gets the Disaster Chef thumbs-up from me.

- 2 tbsp unsalted butter, softened
- 1 egg
- 1 tbsp milk
- ½ tsp vanilla extract
- 4 tbsp self-raising flour
- 2 tbsp caster sugar
- ½ tsp ground cinnamon
- pinch of salt
- 2 heaped tbsp blueberries

1 Put the butter in a large mug.

Any particular mug?

2 Microwave on high for 10–20 seconds until melted. Brush the butter up the sides of the mug to prevent the cake from sticking.

Choose one with straight sides so the cake cooks evenly

Can I use stevia instead of sugar?

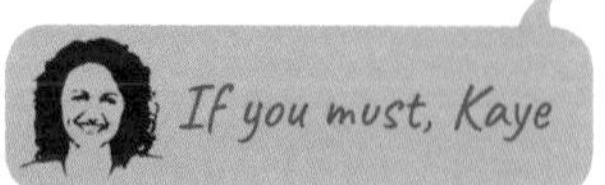

How the heck is anyone supposed to know what is under- or over-whisking? More kitchen witchcraft!

Just beat until it is smooth, there are no lumps, and it's an even colour, then stop

3 Put the egg, milk, and vanilla into the mug and whisk with a fork. Don't over- or under-whisk!

4 Add the flour, sugar, cinnamon, and salt, and give it another whisk until the batter is smooth.

When you're baking, it's important to use measuring spoons, as the quantities really matter

Unless you're making Slapdash Scones (see p132)

Continued >>

5 Gently stir in the blueberries, saving a couple to sprinkle on top.

6 Blast in the microwave for 2 minutes 20 seconds at 600 watts, or 2 minutes at 800 watts, or 1 minute 40 seconds at 1,000 watts.

How can you tell when it's done?

It should be risen and slightly springy to the touch; you can also insert a skewer to the bottom of the mug and, if it comes out clean, it is done

Get it while it's hot

FAFF ALERT
You can dust it with icing sugar before serving if you like.

Healthy-ish Choc Nut Smoothie

Serves 2

NADIA: Kaye and I both have serious chocolate-spread addicts living with us. Yes, Bonnie and Mark, we are talking about you two! The stuff that comes in jars is a bit high in sugar to be truly called healthy, but this might well soothe your cravings.

Make sure you buy the unsweetened nut milk

500ml (16fl oz) hazelnut milk, chilled
3 medjool dates, pitted
2 tbsp cocoa powder

1 Put all the ingredients in a blender and blitz until smooth: almost as good as Nutella... *almost*.

Hack

If you're feeling less virtuous, top this with whipped cream.

Perfect Victoria Sponge

Serves 8

KAYE: Foolproof. I love Victoria sponge! It always makes me think of Sunday afternoons at my granny's house. She made her own and was horrified by shop-bought cake. Sadly, the baking gene got lost somewhere down the line but, come on, just look at that photo... get yer pinny on!

For the cake

4 eggs, weighed in their shells

Now, whatever the eggs weighed, weigh exactly the same amount of:

- soft margarine (from the fridge) or unsalted butter, softened
- caster sugar
- self-raising flour, sifted together with 1 tsp baking powder

1 tbsp milk

1 tsp vanilla extract

For the filling

200ml (7fl oz) double cream

1 tsp vanilla extract

4 tbsp raspberry or strawberry jam

½ tbsp caster sugar, to serve

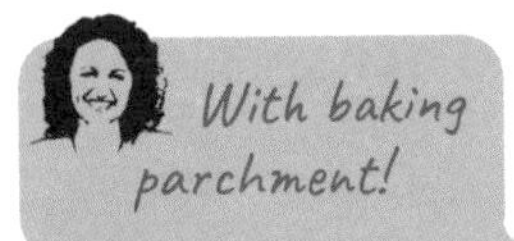

1 Preheat the oven to 160°C (325°F/Gas 3).

2 Grease and line 2 x 20cm (8in) sandwich tins.

Or use easy cake tin liners, if you prefer

3 Put the marg (or butter) and sugar in a bowl, and cream together with a wooden spoon (arm-ache!) or, as I prefer, with an electric whisk.

It's ready when it has almost doubled in volume and lightened to a pale yellowish-white colour

4 Lightly beat the eggs in a small jug, then gradually whisk them into the sugar mixture, beating well after each addition.

Gently!

5 Fold in the flour and baking powder with a metal spoon or spatula.

This is when you can flavour the cake with cocoa, lemon, or orange, and so on

Seems like too much faff to me.

Continued >>

6 Stir in the milk and vanilla, then divide the batter equally between the 2 tins.

7 Bake for 25 minutes on the middle shelf, unless you are using a fan oven, then you can put them anywhere!

8 You know the cakes are done when they are a light golden colour, a little shrunken from the sides, and spring back when you touch them.

9 Remove from the tins and allow to cool completely on a wire rack.

10 When ready to fill the cake, whip the cream with the vanilla extract until thickened. Spread the jam on one of the cakes, then top with the cream and sandwich together with the second cake. Dust with the caster sugar to serve.

To save on washing-up, always make sure you have a Kaye in the kitchen

Marshmallow & Bacon Butty

Makes 1 for a very hungry / greedy person

NADIA: I am unashamed. There are no nutritional benefits whatsoever to this work of the devil but, hey, it's the weekend. Don't ruin it by using wholemeal bread. Plastic white all the way for this one.

You can fry the bacon in a dry frying pan if you prefer, as long as it's crispy – no floppy rashers, please

- 4 rashers of smoked back bacon
- 2 slices of buttered white bread
- 6 marshmallows

1 Grill the bacon until nice and crispy, and lay it on the unbuttered side of one of your slices of bread.

2 Put the marshmallows in the middle of the slice of bread, then lay the second slice of bread on top, butter-side up.

3 Put into a sandwich toaster and cook until light golden brown. (Don't cook it any longer or the marshmallows will leak out and burn.)

What if you haven't got a sandwich toaster?

No problem, just fry it in a dry pan over medium heat, turning once

It is a warped mind that came up with this one

Something Snacky

KAYE: There are some days when a sit-down meal just isn't on the menu. You are either too busy, too disorganized, or – joy of joys – you are home alone and there is no one nipping your ear to ask what's for dinner.

The downside of those days is that the family-sized bag of tortilla chips in the cupboard often starts calling your name rather loudly, so I asked Nadia to come up with a list of "snacky" meals. Tasty, vaguely healthy stuff you can put together without really thinking, and with ingredients you can always have on stand-by. Great, too, when the rest of the family piles in and wants something *now*!

The Pitta Pizza is a firm favourite in my house and will always have a special place in my heart because my youngest loved it so much the first time she tasted it, she didn't realize I had slung some olives on it. Result!

These recipes are all very simple but deceptively delicious. Nadia has a special knack of putting together the right combinations, and I would like to apologize to her now for putting marinated artichokes on everything just because I always have them in the fridge.

Though I am taking full credit for Kaye's Peanut Butter Banana. It's got me through many a long afternoon.

Pitta Pizza

Serves 1

NADIA: A great saviour on a busy week night. I promise, the mayhem caused when I cooked this for Kaye's youngest daughter Bonnie was hard to credit. She loved the pitta pizza so much that she ate a real live olive! Apparently, she's never done it since.

Pop the pitta into a toaster for 30 seconds to soften it first

For the base

1 pitta bread
1 tbsp sun-dried tomato paste or tomato purée
2 tbsp olive oil

For the toppings (all optional)

2 slices of salami or ham, shredded
1 ball of mozzarella, sliced, or 50g (1¾oz) any grated cheese
1 egg (optional)
a couple of black olives (optional)
1 tsp dried oregano or mixed herbs (optional)
basil leaves (optional)

1 Preheat the grill to it highest setting and slice open the pitta bread.

2 Spread the tomato paste equally on the 2 halves.

3 Choose your toppings. Add shredded salami or ham, sliced or grated cheese, or even crack on an egg. Sprinkle with olives, or dried oregano or mixed herbs, or basil leaves, if you like.

4 Drizzle your chosen toppings with a little olive oil and grill until golden and bubbly. This should take 4–7 minutes, but keep an eye on it as you don't want the base or toppings to catch or burn.

Creamy 'Shrooms on Toast

Makes a good meal for 1

NADIA: What a bad, bad wife and mother I am – I wait until they all go out before I make this little pleaser, so I don't have to share it. If you were feeling more generous than me, you could always double the quantities, I suppose.

Don't wash mushrooms: it ruins both their texture and their flavour

Never wash mushrooms? That's the best news I've had all day

- 300g (10oz) mushrooms
- ½ tbsp olive oil
- pinch each of garlic salt and onion salt
- 3 tbsp double cream
- handful of parsley leaves, chopped
- salt and freshly ground black pepper
- 2 slices of your fave bread, toasted and buttered

1 Use a damp piece of kitchen paper to wipe the mushrooms clean. Chop them.

2 Heat the oil over a medium heat in a frying pan. Throw the mushrooms into the oil once it's nice and hot, and keep stirring for a minute or so until they are softened and browned, then add the garlic and onion salt.

3 Stir in the cream and parsley, season, and serve piled on the toast.

Apple & Almond Tower

Makes a snack for 1

NADIA: This is what Kaye and I stuff our faces with when we come in a bit worse for wear (a fairly regular event) or when we are desperate for sugar or chocolate. It heads off the desire to raid the biscuit tin and is pretty healthy, too. Use whatever nut butter is your favourite.

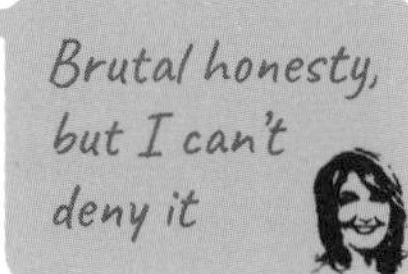

- **1 green apple, unpeeled**
- **1 red apple, unpeeled**
- **2 tbsp almond, peanut or cashew butter**

1 Simply core and slice the apples, and spread alternate layers of each apple with whatever nut butter tickles your fancy!

A brilliant way of keeping the kids away from the biscuit tin. For some reason, an apple and almond tower is more enticing than chucking them a Granny Smith and a tub of peanut butter

Hack

Another option that works just as well is a ripe sliced Conference pear with cashew butter.

S.O.S. Salmon Supper

Makes a snack for 1

KAYE: This is a great little supper if you literally only have minutes to prepare something edible and feed yourself before you're back out of the door – whose idea was it to take them to Scouts at 6.30 on a Tuesday evening anyway?

- 2 tbsp cream cheese
- 2 seeded crispbreads
- 4 slices of smoked salmon or smoked trout
- 1 tbsp toasted pumpkin seeds
- lemon juice, to serve
- freshly ground black pepper

1 Spread the cream cheese equally between the crispbreads, then top with the slices of salmon or trout and the pumpkin seeds.

2 Finish with a squeeze of lemon juice and a twist of black pepper. Eat.

Can be followed by a double choc muffin, but not essential

Lemony Sardines on Toast

Serves 1

NADIA: I felt embarrassed at Kaye's over-exuberant delight the first time I knocked up this little fishy dishy for us. Complete satisfaction in a can, sardines are protein-rich and keep you feeling full for ages.

How could I have reached this age and never thought to open a can of sardines? Is it sad to admit they take me to a happy place?

135g can sardines (I like Parmentier lemon sardines)
squeeze of lemon juice (if you've got some)
splash of Tabasco (again, only if you've got some)
2 slices of your fave bread, lightly toasted
handful of watercress or spinach
freshly ground black pepper

1 Put the sardines with their oil into a bowl and break them up a bit with a fork.

But don't mush them completely, this isn't fish paste

2 Squeeze the lemon juice (if using) on top, then splash in the Tabasco (if using). Give it a stir.

3 Pile the mixture onto the toast.

4 Top with the watercress or spinach, then season with lots of pepper.

Faff alert

As you can see from the photo, I would add quartered cherry tomatoes and lemon wedges, for squeezing. Kaye would not.

Faff-free Guacamole

Serves 4

NADIA: This is as basic as I get! I would usually add freshly chopped tomatoes but Kaye demanded faff-free guac for you all, and her wish is my command! Even this unfussy version is about a hundred times better than the awful shop-bought green mush she used to eat.

2 ripe avocados

pinch of chilli flakes, or 1 small red chilli, finely sliced

good pinch each of garlic salt and onion salt

1 tbsp chopped coriander

finely grated zest and juice of 1 small lime

½ tbsp olive oil

Hack

Limes can be really stubborn to juice but if you roll them firmly on a work surface before you cut into them, they will release loads more liquid.

1 Pit, peel, and chop the avocados. Put them in a bowl with all the other ingredients, then mix and mash a little using a fork. Make it as smooth or as chunky as you like.

2 Serve with whatever you fancy! We photographed them with toasted tortilla wraps.

Can I suggest oatcakes, oatcakes, or oatcakes?

I make this when I've got avocados going a bit mushy. This little bit of titillation makes me feel like I am whipping up a savoury treat rather than saving stuff from the bin

Kaye's Peanut Butter Banana

Serves… a purpose

KAYE: Now, even I don't have the nerve to call this a recipe. Can a recipe have only two ingredients? Let's call it a killer combo. Take it seriously, though, and treat it with respect: many of those who worked on this book are now addicted to it! This is my go-to snack after a long dog walk or workout.

1 firm banana
your favourite peanut butter

None of your black ones from the bottom of the fruit bowl

1. Take the banana.
2. Peel it.
3. Slice it in half lengthways.
4. Spread peanut butter on the cut edge and sandwich the banana together.
5. Bob's your uncle, Fanny's your aunt!

Something Up Your Sleeve

KAYE: If you want to know if someone is a Disaster Chef or a kitchen natural, do a spot-check of their fridge. Nadia's is always overflowing. Not one kind of cheese but five. Every variety of nut there is – apparently you are supposed to keep them chilled, who knew?

She has types of vegetable I didn't realize existed and lorry-loads of organic beef, steak, ham, partridge, guinea fowl, spatchcocked chicken… you get the picture. There isn't one millimetre of spare space.

Cut to mine. There will always be at least one day when it looks like a nuclear winter. I'll have forgotten to do the online shop or the week will have run away with me and we'll be down to an egg, half a tub of mouldy cream cheese, an onion, and a single probiotic yogurt. It's clearly time to pull out the recipes in this chapter.

Pasta Puttanesca is a lifesaver. It seriously tastes like one of those simple little dishes you're served at a country osteria during your road trip to Tuscany, and you bore the pants off your friends for weeks afterwards telling them about it. (Not that I've ever done a road trip to Tuscany, but I've seen one on the telly.)

I'd recommend packaging up the ingredients for all the recipes in this chapter and putting them in a cool dark place in a box with a red cross on it. Emergency supplies.

Easiest Spaghetti Ever

Serves 4

NADIA: Kaye tries to pretend she doesn't eat pasta. She never quite manages to maintain that deceit when there's a pot of this on the stove. I have never met a person that hasn't loved this dish, and it's done and on the table within 10 minutes. Storecupboard heaven!

She's right – I could eat a bucket of it

sea salt and freshly ground black pepper
500g packet of dried spaghetti
3 tbsp olive oil
1 garlic clove, crushed
3 tbsp tomato purée or sun-dried tomato paste
grated Parmesan cheese (optional)
basil leaves (optional)

Hack

Always salt pasta water really well. It needs more than you think: it makes the difference between tasteless, flabby pasta, and sublime spaghetti.

1 Fill the largest pan you have with boiling water, then add enough salt until it tastes as salty as the sea. Cook the spaghetti for as long as it says on the packet.

2 Meanwhile, pour the olive oil into a large non-stick frying pan and place over a low heat. Add the garlic but keep the heat low and stir until translucent. *Do not overcook the garlic* or you'll ruin the dish.

3 Add the tomato purée or sun-dried tomato paste and fry, stirring the whole time, for 1 minute. Season with salt and pepper, and fry for another 20 seconds. Don't worry if it looks odd.

4 Take a ladleful of pasta cooking water (about 150ml / 5fl oz), add it to the pan and stir until well mixed. Then turn the heat off.

5 Once the cooking time is up on the spaghetti, drain it and add it to the frying pan. Toss the spaghetti until it is nicely coated with the sauce.

6 Ready to serve. You can, of course, add grated Parmesan cheese and basil leaves, if some are knocking about, although we don't usually bother.

Tuna Quinoa Salad

Serves 4-6

NADIA: Not only is this a great storecupboard recipe but it's one that is smart enough (and trendy enough) to serve to friends as well. Kaye loves this – her body's her temple, you know!

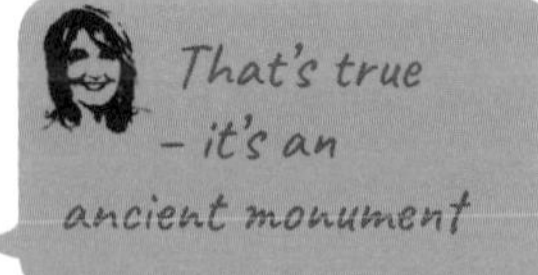

For the salad

- 2 x 250g bags pre-cooked quinoa
- 200g can tuna, drained and flaked
- 280g jar chargrilled peppers, drained and chopped
- 20 black olives
- 100g (3½oz) canned haricot or kidney beans, drained and rinsed
- handful of parsley, mint, or basil leaves, finely chopped

You can add two if you like lots!

For the dressing

- 1 tsp Dijon mustard
- 3 tbsp olive oil
- 1½ tbsp tahini
- ½ garlic clove, crushed
- ½ tsp honey
- pinch of caster sugar
- finely grated zest of ½ unwaxed lemon
- 2½ tbsp lemon juice
- salt

When I add the tahini to the dressing, it goes all claggy

Never fear – just keep whisking, and add a splash of water if you like, and it will become smooth again

1 Put all the dressing ingredients in a bowl with a good pinch of salt, and whisk until smooth. Set aside.

2 Put the quinoa in a serving bowl along with the tuna, peppers, olives, haricot or kidney beans, and herbs.

Continued >>

It's important to quality-check the olives

3 Drizzle the dressing over. Very gently mix all the ingredients without breaking up the chunks of tuna or the beans too much. Make sure the dressing evenly coats all the elements of the salad.

4 If you have any dressing left, you can keep it in the fridge for up to 5 days in a sealed jar.

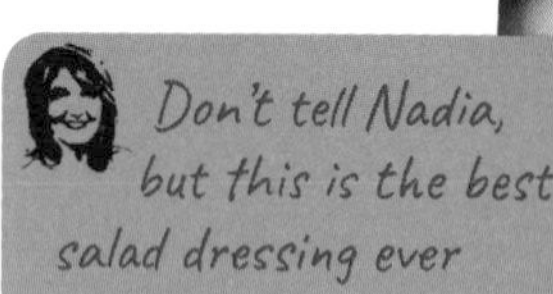

HACK
Griddled halloumi or chicken would be nice instead of the tuna, for a change.

My Own Mac & Cheese

Serves 4

KAYE: This is a huge favourite in our house. The mustard and bacon add a bit of zing and, goodness knows why, making individual servings feels kinda posh! It's economical, too, so is a good one to have up your sleeve as you approach the yawning gap in the lead-up to pay day.

Or you can use any pasta shapes you happen to have in the cupboard

- 225g (8oz) macaroni
- 480g jar good-quality béchamel sauce
- 250g (9oz) grated frozen mature Cheddar cheese
- 1 heaped tsp Dijon mustard
- 150g (5½oz) frozen bacon lardons
- 50g (1¾oz) grated Parmesan cheese

Faff alert

If you like, you can pre-cook the bacon lardons by frying them in a dry frying pan until crisp and golden.

1. Cook the macaroni according to the packet instructions.
2. Meanwhile, pour the béchamel sauce into a saucepan and place it over a medium-low heat.
3. Put 200g (7oz) of the Cheddar cheese and the mustard into the sauce, and stir well until smooth.
4. Preheat the grill on the highest setting.
5. When the macaroni is cooked, drain it very well, then return it to the pan. Pour the cheesed-up sauce over it and mix well.
6. Divide between 4 ovenproof dishes, each about 15 x 9cm (6 x 3½in).
7. Sprinkle the lardons evenly between the dishes, then scatter with the remaining Cheddar and the Parmesan.
8. Pop under the hot grill. It is ready when the cheese is brown and bubbly. That won't take longer than 5 minutes, so keep an eye on it and don't leave the kitchen or take a phone call.

Cashew & Cauli Curry

Serves 4

KAYE: Believe it or not, Nadia's not the only one to have appeared on *Celebrity MasterChef*. I also made a (brief) appearance, which you may have missed if you happened to blink. According to the judges, my curry wasn't hot enough. What do they know? I don't like hot food. It's your kitchen and your mouth: make this as hot or mild as you like.

I hate this, so would use 4 garlic cloves, chopped

- 80g (2¾oz) cashew nuts
- 2 tbsp vegetable oil
- 200g (7oz) frozen onions, or 3 fresh onions, sliced
- 1–2 tsp garlic paste, from a jar
- 4 tbsp madras or korma curry paste (not sauce)
- 600g (1lb 5oz) frozen cauliflower, cut into similar-sized pieces
- 400ml can full-fat coconut milk
- salt
- 50g (1¾oz) raisins or sultanas
- 200g (7oz) frozen spinach, defrosted
- 3 tsp nigella seeds (onion seeds)
- 4–8 tbsp Greek yogurt
- wraps, to serve

1 Tip the cashews into a dry frying pan and set it over a medium heat, stirring, until the nuts are toasted. Tip them out into a small bowl and set aside.

2 Heat the oil over a medium heat in a large pan and fry the onions and garlic until softened.

3 Add the curry paste and fry for 2 minutes, stirring, then add the cauliflower and fry, stirring, for 1 more minute.

4 Now pour in the coconut milk and bring up to the bubble for a minute. Add a good pinch of salt.

5 Reduce the heat, add the raisins or sultanas, then simmer for 10–12 minutes, or until the cauli is tender and the sauce has thickened a little.

6 Stir in the spinach to wilt. Top with the toasted cashew nuts and the nigella seeds. Serve with yogurt and wraps (rice or potatoes are also good).

Pasta Puttanesca

Serves 4

KAYE: Punchy, authentic, and quicker than a takeaway, this is on your plate in 30 minutes. Even better, every ingredient could have been hanging about at the back of your cupboard since Christmas.

- 400–500g (14oz–1lb 2oz) dried spaghetti
- 4 tbsp good olive oil
- 4–6 garlic cloves, thinly sliced (if you can't be bothered, crushed are OK)
- 80g tin or jar anchovy fillets in olive oil
- ½ tsp chilli flakes (optional)
- 10 good-quality black olives, roughly chopped
- 1 tbsp capers in brine, rinsed (or they will be too salty)
- 2 tbsp tomato purée
- 400ml (14fl oz) tomato passata, or 400g can can chopped tomatoes
- salt and freshly ground black pepper
- basil leaves (optional)

When cooking Italian, it's important to compare the size of your pepper grinders

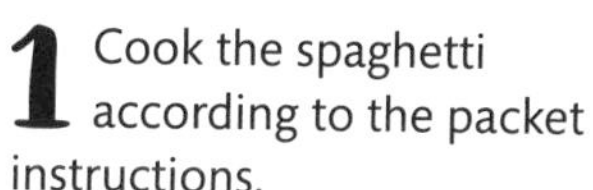

1 Cook the spaghetti according to the packet instructions.

2 Meanwhile, heat the oil over a medium heat in a heavy-based frying pan. Add the garlic and cook until transparent, then add the anchovies and stir.

Bash the anchovies until they break up and dissolve

I didn't believe her, but the anchovies actually do dissolve

3 Add the chilli (if using), olives, and capers, and increase the heat a bit until you hear a sizzle. Add the tomato purée and fry it in the pan, stirring, then add the passata or canned tomatoes, and bring to the boil. Let it bubble for 3–4 minutes. Taste and add salt and pepper.

Continued >>

You need to cook tomato purée, passata, and canned tomatoes, or they will taste raw

As you can see, this dish is difficult so I had to concentrate really hard. Not

4 Drain the spaghetti and add to the pan. Toss well. Serve with lots of basil if you have any. I didn't (see pic).

You can add more chilli if you like it spicy

Fabulous Fish Stew

Serves 4

ADIA: This one is truly great. Just raid the freezer and vegetable rack, and you're there. Easy to bung together even on a busy Wednesday night, and something of a crowd-pleaser, but it always feels like a treat.

Actually, I'd go for fabulous. I can do this one in 20 minutes flat from opening the freezer

door to clearing my plate. Stupendous

- tbsp olive oil
- large onions, sliced
- garlic cloves, crushed
- 00ml (3½fl oz) dry white wine
- 00g can chopped tomatoes
- 00ml (14fl oz) vegetable, ish, or chicken stock
- heaped tsp dried oregano
- alt and freshly ground black epper
- 00g (1lb 2oz) frozen chunky white ish fillets, defrosted
- 00g (7oz) frozen raw prawns, efrosted
- andful of black olives (optional)
- ustic bread, or 1 stick of frozen arlic bread, to serve

1 Heat the oil in a heavy-based wide saucepan or sauté pan over a medium heat.

2 Throw in the onions and garlic, and fry until softened but not browned. Increase the heat a bit, pour in the wine, and let it bubble for 30 seconds.

3 Add the tomatoes, stock, and oregano, bring to the boil, then reduce the heat to a simmer and place the pan over a heat diffuser (see p13). Season with salt and pepper.

Why should I leave the lid off?

4 Simmer over a medium-low heat, with the lid off, for 8–10 minutes, or until the sauce is thick enough to coat the fillets. Stir now and again.

So the juices can evaporate, to make a thicker sauce

5 Cut the fish into large chunks, add to the pan, cover, and simmer very gently for 4–5 minutes.

6 Add the prawns and cook until they turn pink. Throw in the olives (if using), just until they have warmed through. Don't overcook the fish. Stop now!

7 Serve the stew with rustic bread to mop up the sauce, or with garlic bread (if using), heated according to the packet instructions.

Something Cheaty

KAYE: Nadia calls it "cheaty" because she is a purist. I am a pragmatist, so I call it smart. Tell me, why would I spend hours of my life and several notches on my blood pressure levels trying to make a flan case? Or raspberry ripple ice cream? Or puff pastry from scratch?

As a Disaster Chef, I'll do my best to turn out tasty, healthy food for the family, but if someone chucks me a rope and offers to drag me out of the water, I won't refuse.

So, what we have here are some seriously classy-looking and delicious dishes which, with the help of a few ready-made ingredients, punch way above their weight.

Spaghetti Vongole followed by Pimped-up Pandoro would qualify as a Christmas dinner in my book, yet they've only got six or seven ingredients apiece, and one of them is alcohol. Required skill level? Negligible.

I am in awe of Nadia's talents in the kitchen and, in particular, envy the sheer joy she gets from cooking. Who knows, with a bit more practice and a bit more success, I might one day think, "Can't wait to get home and get my pinny on". But, until that day, I am going to take all the help I can get.

A Cheating Tart

Serves 4-6

KAYE: OK, I'll fess up. I haven't actually made this one yet, but I *can* say that I walked into Nadia's house last week, starving, and there was one of these, fresh out of the oven. Bloomin' gorgeous. I seriously thought she'd bought it from a posh little French deli. And all you have to do, fellow Disaster Chefs, is open some jars and packets. Result.

My husband Mark named this recipe – what could he mean?

320g pack ready-rolled puff pastry
a little milk
4 tbsp pesto
285g jar artichoke hearts in olive oil, drained
285g jar roasted peppers, drained
1 ball of mozzarella, very well drained and torn
a little olive oil (optional)
1 tsp dried oregano

Faff alert

Slice 2 cloves of garlic thinly, drizzle in oil and scatter on the top for the last couple of minutes of baking time.

1 Preheat the oven to 220°C (425°F/Gas 7).

2 Unroll the puff pastry on a baking tray, leaving it in the greaseproof paper it came in, and, with the tip of a sharp knife, score a 2–3cm (¾–1¼in) margin around the edge on all sides. Be careful not to cut all the way through.

3 Brush the pastry margin with the milk, then spread the pesto on the pastry within the margin.

4 Scatter the artichokes evenly on top, still inside the margin, along with the peppers.

5 Top with the torn mozzarella and a drizzle of olive oil, then sprinkle evenly with the oregano.

6 Bake for 20 minutes, or until the cheese is bubbling. Allow to cool a little before serving. Don't tell a soul everything came out of a jar.

Use the oil that is left in the jars of artichokes or peppers

This is my kind of cooking – food assembly! I'm hoping it will catch on

Spaghetti Vongole

Serves 4

KAYE: I admit, when we were shooting these pictures, I was turning my nose up, but I wolfed the lot. This really punches above its weight. The sauce is so flavoursome – one of my favourites. I now have a wee stash of jars of clams always on hand which, for a girl brought up on spaghetti hoops and toast, is quite something.

- 4 tbsp olive oil
- 6 garlic cloves, crushed
- 400g can chopped tomatoes in juice
- 450g (1lb) dried spaghetti
- 2 x 250g jars clams in brine (vongole), drained
- salt and freshly ground black pepper
- handful of parsley leaves, chopped (optional)

1 Pour the oil into a heavy-based frying pan over a medium heat. Fry the garlic, stirring the whole time, until translucent but not brown.

2 Now tip in the chopped tomatoes and cook over a medium-low heat, uncovered, for 15 minutes, or until the oil and tomatoes have separated.

Kaye bought whole not chopped tomatoes, so I made her chop them in the pan

I didn't even realise canned tomatoes could be "the wrong ones"

3 After the tomato sauce has been cooking for about 10 minutes, cook the spaghetti according to the packet instructions.

When the oil separates from the sauce, it's a sign that the tomatoes are cooked

Continued >>

4 Once the tomato sauce is cooked, add the clams and cook gently until heated through, seasoning well.

What clams should I buy?

Look for clams in brine: they often come in a can, which is fine, but the best ones are in a jar. If you can't find them, you can use tuna instead

5 Drain the pasta, add it to the sauce, and toss very well.

6 If you have some parsley, stir it in now. Please find some!

There's an art to tossing pasta with sauce: clamp a lid on, pick up the pan, and toss it all about pretty violently

A truly excellent fishy cheat treat!

Creamy Chicken & Mushroom Pie

Serves 4

KAYE: This is my kind of recipe. No fancy-nancy ingredients, 10 minutes prep, then whack it in the oven. Plenty of time to go and check your emails and stick on a wash. Also dead easy to scale up or down. This gets the Disaster Chef seal of approval.

- 1 egg, lightly beaten
- splash of milk
- salt
- 500g (1lb 2oz) cooked chicken
- 295g can cream of mushroom soup
- 1 tsp Dijon mustard
- 320g pack ready-rolled puff pastry

Faff alert

As you can see from the photo, when I make it, I fry a handful each of leeks and mushrooms until soft, and add to the chicken. Worth it!

Hack

The filling ingredients should be cold or the pastry will melt!

I didn't know pastry could melt, stop making me nervous

1. Preheat the oven to 200°C (400°F/Gas 6).
2. Whisk the egg, milk, and salt together in a small bowl and set aside.
3. Tear the chicken up and put it in a 23cm (9in) pie dish. Pour the soup into a bowl and mix in the mustard, then pour this mixture over the chicken.
4. Brush a little egg mixture around the edge of the pie dish. Lay the pastry on top, pushing it down onto the rim, and brush it, too, with the egg mixture.
5. Using a sharp knife, make a small hole in the centre of the pastry.
6. Bake for 30–35 minutes, or until the pastry is puffed up and golden. Serve with peas.

Why would I make a hole in the pastry?

To let the steam out - don't skip this step or you will have soggy pastry!

Pimped-up Pandoro

Serves 6–8

KAYE: This sweet sculpture is thing of beauty. If only your guests knew just how easy it was to make… shhhhh. Not only is it delicious, it gladdens my Scottish heart because it means no more wasted pandoro at Christmas time. I love to get them as gifts but there's only so much Italian cake you can have with a cup of tea.

From the supermarket or an Italian deli

- 1 large pandoro
- 200ml (7fl oz) your favourite liqueur
- 300ml (10fl oz) double cream
- 250g (9oz) mascarpone
- finely grated zest of 1 unwaxed lemon
- 500g (1lb 2oz) of mixed berries, such as raspberries, strawberries, and blueberries

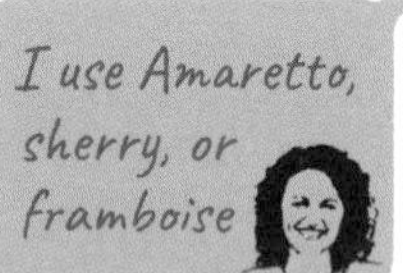

Can I use whisky? Or Irn-Bru?

1 Cut the pandoro horizontally into 4 slices. Set aside 2 tbsp from the packet of icing sugar you'll find inside the box, then tip the rest into a large bowl.

Is there a trick to this?

Use a serrated bread knife and go s l o w l y

2 Pour the liqueur onto a large plate or shallow dish.

We don't want to soak them, just imbue them with alcohol

3 Very briskly dip each slice of cake into the liqueur. Set aside.

4 Put the cream, mascarpone, and lemon zest into the large bowl with the icing sugar, and whisk until you have soft peaks.

This is easier with an electric whisk but you can use a hand whisk

How do you dunk pandoro?

Continued >>

5 Divide the mascarpone mixture between the 4 slices of pandoro, starting with the biggest slice and stacking the layers up on a serving plate.

6 Scatter a few raspberries and blueberries on each layer where the points stick out, after you stack them.

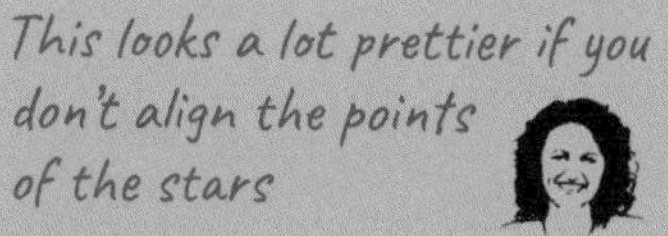

Far be it from me, but a few chocolate buttons scattered about make it even more scrumptious

7 Scatter the remaining berries on top of the cake and around the serving plate.

8 Give it a good dusting with the reserved 2 tbsp of icing sugar.

Use a sieve and dust over the icing sugar from a height, to give an even dusting

HACK

Panettone will work brilliantly, too, minus the starry effect.

Chocolate Croissant Pudding

Serves 6

KAYE: Easy peasy though this is, I have to confess I am tempted just to dip the pains au chocolat in the custard and save myself the washing up – but that's for those "home-alone" evenings. This has the potential to impress, so go the whole hog and switch the oven on.

unsalted butter, for greasing
6 pains au chocolat
500g best-quality vanilla custard
150ml (5fl oz) whole milk

I asked Nadia if I could used skimmed milk and she stamped on my foot – I take it that's a "no"

1 Lightly butter an oven dish, then lay the pains au chocolat in the dish.

2 Mix the custard and milk together, and pour over the pains au chocolat. Leave for 30 minutes for the custard to soak into the pains au chocolat.

3 Preheat the oven to 160°C (325°F/Gas 3). Put the dish in a deep baking tray and fill the tray with hot water until the water reaches to halfway up the dish. (Don't splash any water in the pudding.)

4 Bake for 30–35 minutes. Leave to settle for 10 minutes, then serve.

Why should you leave it hanging around?

Don't skip this step – it makes for a custardy, luscious pudding rather than a runny, separated sauce – just keep it away from the dog...

Birthday Baked Alaska

Serves very many

KAYE: No more sobbing in the kitchen on the eve of your little darling's birthday – this is a cake you *can* make! Fellow Disaster Chefs, do not freak when you see the word "meringue". It really is a lot easier than I ever imagined, but follow the steps to the letter. It is tempting to whack the whisk straight up to high speed: resist.

For the base

900ml (1½ pints) raspberry ripple soft-scoop ice cream
24cm (9½in) ready-made sponge flan base

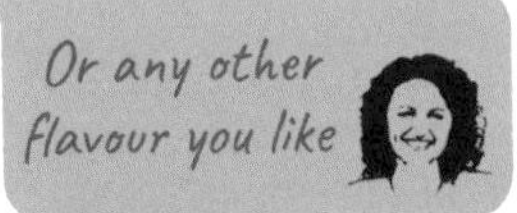

Or any other flavour you like

For the meringue

a little vinegar or lemon juice
4 large eggs
240g (8½oz) caster sugar

1 Line a 23cm (9in) diameter pudding basin with a double layer of cling film. Spoon the ice cream into it, pressing down so you have an inverted dome shape with a smooth, level top surface. Fold in the cling film to cover and return to the freezer.

If the ice cream isn't soft-scoop, let it soften for 30 minutes before trying to mould it

2 Preheat the oven to 220°C (425°F/Gas 7). While it's heating up, make the meringue.

3 Clean a large metal or glass bowl (not plastic) with a little vinegar or lemon juice (see p248).

Go on, I'll bite: how do I do this?

Crack an egg over a bowl; catch the yolk in your fingers or in the shell, letting the white run through. Slip the yolk into another bowl

4 Separate the eggs. Set aside the yolks for another recipe.

5 Put the egg whites into your gorgeously clean bowl.

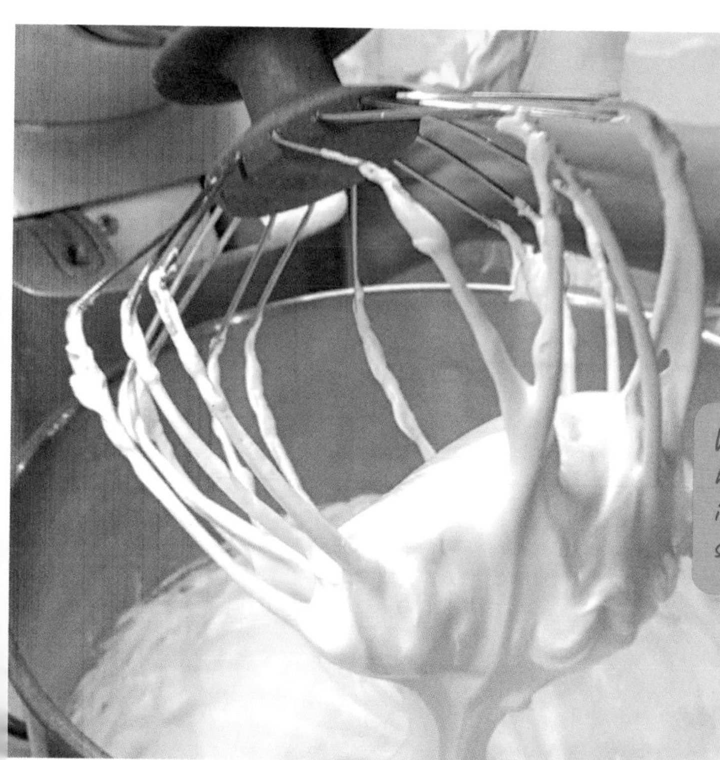

6 Using an electric whisk, whisk the whites on a low speed. Gradually increase the speed to medium until they form soft peaks.

7 Increase the speed of your whisk to its highest setting. Then, whisking continuously, add the sugar, a spoon at a time, until the meringue is shiny and holds stiff peaks.

Why do you have to add it so tortuously slowly?

So that the sugar is properly dissolved, therefore avoiding grainy meringue

Continued >>

8 Take the ice cream bowl out of the freezer. Put the flan base on a baking tray lined with baking parchment. With the help of the cling film, pull the ice cream out of the bowl and put it dome-side up on the flan base. Remove all the cling film.

9 Quickly spoon the meringue over the ice cream and flan, right down to the baking parchment, making pretty peaks as you go.

Why does the meringue have to go down to the parchment?

To seal the whole thing, or the ice cream will leak!

10 Put into the centre of your hot oven and cook for 4 minutes, or until the meringue is set and light golden in colour.

11 Carefully transfer the Alaska to a serving plate... if you can wait.

I nearly cried when I took this out the oven and it actually looked like the picture, I don't think that's ever happened before

We think those are happy birthday-girl faces

Something Sweet

KAYE: This might come as a bit of a surprise, but I rather enjoy a spot of baking. I find it very therapeutic. Strangely enough, it was my elder daughter who got me into it. She started with chocolate crispie cakes when she was pre-school, and carried on from there. Now, if we come home and smell that wonderful aroma of baking, we know that whatever I've dished up for tea, we are in for a treat afterwards.

It's in stark contrast to my own childhood. My dear mum's one and only attempt at scones was true Disaster Chef. Not only did they not rise, they sank. When they came out of the oven, they looked for all the world like a tray of biscuits.

I am somewhere in the middle but what I love about baking or making a sweet treat is that there isn't the same level of expectation. If it works, that's a bonus. If it doesn't, it might be a disappointment, but you're not going to go hungry and you can console yourself that you've saved a few calories. Or is that just my warped mindset?

Anyway, you are unlikely to go wrong with these recipes; they are ridiculously easy. And yes, it is obligatory to drink a G&T to go along with the Lemon Gin & Tonic Cake, either while making it or eating it. Or both. It would be rude not to.

Crazy Easy Apple Tart

Serves 6

NADIA: Trust me, this is so ridiculously easy that I've felt the need to add an extra faffy bit with the Chantilly cream accompaniment, but you can of course just use pouring, clotted, or whipping cream instead. Just not squirty cream, please!

For the tart

- 320g pack ready-rolled puff pastry
- 1 egg
- 1 tbsp milk
- small pinch of salt
- 60g (2¼oz) unsalted butter
- 1 heaped tsp ground cinnamon
- 3 Granny Smith apples
- 4 tbsp granulated sugar

For the Chantilly cream

- 200ml (7fl oz) double cream or whipping cream
- 40g (1½oz) icing sugar
- 1 tsp vanilla extract
- 1 tbsp Calvados (optional)

Hack

Take the pastry out of the fridge 10 minutes before you start, or it will be too brittle to unroll.

1 Make sure your pastry is out of the fridge (see below). Preheat the oven to 200°C (400°F/Gas 6). Line a baking tray with baking parchment. Make the egg wash by lightly beating the egg in a cup, adding the milk and salt. (The salt breaks down the protein in the egg so it is easier to brush.) Set aside.

2 Cut the pastry lengthwise into 2 long strips and return to the fridge. Melt the butter in a small pan, mix in the cinnamon, and allow to cool a little.

3 Remove the apple cores with a corer (see p13), then peel the apples and slice into thin rings. Place in a bowl and toss with the cinnamon butter.

4 Arrange the apples on each piece of pastry, overlapping them slightly but leaving a 2cm (¾in) border around the edge. Sprinkle them with the sugar. Brush the pastry with the egg wash, then bake for 20–25 minutes, or until lightly golden.

5 For the Chantilly cream, put the cream and icing sugar in a bowl. Using an electric whisk, whisk until you get soft peaks. Add the vanilla and the booze (if using) and give it a stir. Voilà – posh cream to serve with your tart!

Is there a right way to line a baking tray?

I dot butter on each corner of the tray, then lay parchment on top. The butter keeps it in place

Don't over-whisk; better to stop early than too late

Blackberry & Apple Loaf

Makes about 8 slices

ADIA: We have my big sister Dina to thank for this recipe. It's a bit f an odd method for a cake because she rubs the butter into the our, but I'm pretty scared of my big sis so would never dare to uestion her. It tastes completely lovely anyway.

- 75g (6oz) unsalted butter, ftened, plus extra for greasing
- 50g (9oz) self-raising flour
- tsp baking powder
- 00g (3½oz) muscovado or ster sugar
- 00g (3½oz) caster sugar
- heaped tsp ground cinnamon
- large eggs, lightly beaten
- nely grated zest of unwaxed lemon
- small eating apple, peeled d grated
- 25g (8oz) blackberries (fine to use nned, no one will ever know!)

Hack

Check the cake halfway through and, if it looks like it's getting brown too quickly, loosely cover it with foil.

1 Preheat the oven to 180°C (350°F/Gas 4). Line a 900g (2lb) loaf tin with a strip of baking parchment long enough to hang over each end of the tin. This will help you pull the loaf out later. Line the base with more baking parchment.

2 Sift the flour and baking powder together into a bowl. Add the sugars and cinnamon.

3 Rub the softened butter into the mixture until it forms fine crumbs. Set aside.

4 Put the eggs in a separate bowl and stir in the lemon zest and apple.

5 Make a well in the flour mixture and quickly stir in the egg and apple mixture. Fold in two-thirds of the blackberries, then spoon the batter into the prepared tin and sprinkle the remaining berries on top.

6 Bake for 1 hour, then insert a skewer into the centre of the cake: if it comes out clean, the loaf cake is ready. Allow to cool in the tin for 5 minutes, then turn out onto a cake rack by pulling on the baking parchment strip. Make sure to leave the cake baked-side up. Leave until completely cold – if you have that much self-control.

If you can't be bothered to sift them, mix the baking powder and flour around a bit with your fingers

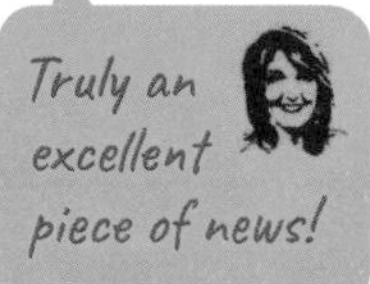

Lemon Gin & Tonic Cake

Makes about 8 good-sized slices

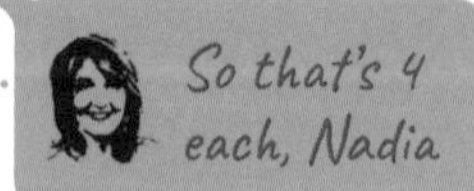

KAYE: A tipsy twist on the classic lemon drizzle. What can I say, except: any excuse, any bloody excuse. I actually watched Nadia make this last week, while sinking quite a bit more gin than she put in the cake. Make ours a large one.

For the cake

- 200g (7oz) softened unsalted butter, plus extra for greasing
- 175g (6oz) caster sugar
- 4 medium eggs
- 200g (7oz) self-raising flour
- ½ tsp baking powder
- finely grated zest of 1 unwaxed lemon
- 75ml (2½fl oz) gin

For the syrup

- 60g (2oz) caster sugar
- 60ml (2fl oz) tonic water
- 2 tbsp gin

For the icing and decoration

- 50g (1¾oz) granulated sugar
- juice of ½ lemon
- 1 tsp gin
- 1 lemon, very finely sliced with a mandoline

1 Preheat the oven to 180°C (350°F/Gas 4).

2 Butter a 900g loaf tin and line the base and sides with baking parchment.

3 Put the butter and sugar into a bowl, and whisk with an electric whisk until pale, light, and fluffy.

How long do I have to stand here and do this?

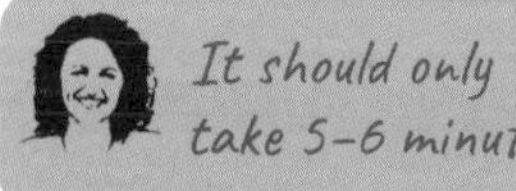

4 Lightly beat the eggs in a jug. You just need them to all become the same iform, yellow colour.

5 Pour them, bit by bit, into the butter and sugar mixture, whisking all the while.

6 Gently fold in the flour, baking powder, and lemon zest, so you don't burst the air ibbles in the batter. Pour in the gin and give a gentle stir. Spoon into the prepared tin.

How do I know when the sugar has dissolved?

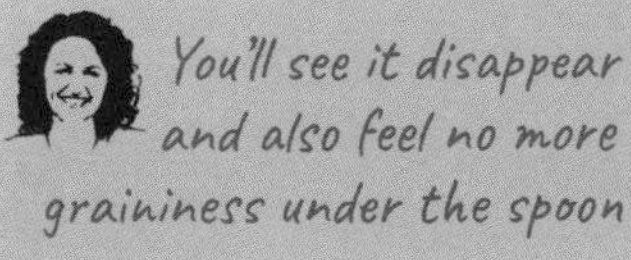

7 Bake for 1 hour. After 55 minutes, insert a skewer into the centre of the cake and, if it comes out clean, take the cake out of the oven. If it doesn't, give it another 5 minutes.

8 Meanwhile, make the syrup. Put the sugar and tonic water into a small pan and set over a low heat.

9 Stir until the sugar dissolves.

10 Increase the heat and boil the syrup for 1 minute without stirring.

11 Measure out 2 tbsp of the syrup into a small bowl and mix in the gin. (Discard the remaining syrup.)

Continued >>

12 Once the cake is out of the oven, use a skewer to make 8 holes in it.

13 Drizzle the gin syrup over the top of the cake and leave to cool in the tin.

14 Turn out the cake, turn it right-side up again, and place on a wire rack.

15 Mix together the ingredients for the icing and spoon it on the cake. Arrange the lemon slices along the top. Leave to set.

16 Eat. With a glass of G&T alongside... naturally.

HACK

To fold in flour, use a metal spoon or rubber spatula to cut down through the batter, then do a “lift and over” motion. Give the bowl a quarter-turn and repeat.

Austrian Berry Pancake

Serves 4

KAYE: Quite frankly, I don't know how this recipe slipped through the net. The minute I saw the reference to "butter shavings", my eyes rolled back in my head. Baked plums? I've never baked a plum in my life! However, some of you may be a few levels up from my Disaster Chef status, so crack on, it sounds delicious.

- 1 tbsp raisins
- 2 tbsp rum, brandy, or Marsala
- 3 eggs
- pinch of salt
- 2 tsp caster sugar
- 150ml (5fl oz) whole milk
- 175g (6oz) plain flour
- 2 tbsp unsalted butter, plus 1 tbsp butter shavings (see below)
- 1 tbsp granulated sugar
- ½ tbsp icing sugar
- ½ tsp ground cinnamon
- handful of mixed berries, baked plums, or fruit compote, if you prefer
- custard or cream, to serve

Hack

Make fancy butter shavings by using a potato peeler to shave a block of frozen butter.

1 Preheat the oven to 180°C (350°F/Gas 4). Put the raisins in a small bowl and pour over the alcohol you've chosen. Leave for up to 2 hours (10 minutes is the minimum), then drain.

2 Separate the eggs (see p209). Add a pinch of salt to the egg whites and, using an electric whisk, whisk until they hold stiff peaks (see p249).

3 In another bowl, with a clean electric whisk, whisk the egg yolks with the caster sugar, then whisk in the milk and flour to make a smooth batter. Add the egg whites and gently mix in.

4 In an ovenproof frying pan, melt the 2 tbsp butter over a medium-low heat until bubbling. Pour in the batter. After a couple of minutes, scatter the drained raisins on top. Cook for 3–4 minutes over a very low heat. Using a spatula, lift a corner of the pancake; when it's light brown underneath, turn it over.

5 Put in the oven for 6–8 minutes until nicely golden. Remove from the oven. Turn the grill on to high.

6 Cut the pancake into small pieces with scissors, return to the pan, scatter butter shavings over the top, and sprinkle with the granulated sugar. Put under the grill to caramelize.

7 Meanwhile, mix the icing sugar and cinnamon in a bowl. When the pancake has caramelized, dust with the icing sugar mixture. Serve with fruit, and custard or cream... or both!

The pancake will turn golden brown and you will smell caramel

Strawberry Grand Marnier Crumble

Serves 4

KAYE: Why has no one thought of this before? Cooking crumble like this means you can get it just as you like it, whether that's soft or crunchy and golden. This really is the best way to make crumble but I have to put out a warning because it's oh-so-pickable. Don't end up eating it all!

For the filling

400g (14oz) strawberries
1 tbsp caster sugar
2 tbsp Grand Marnier

For the crumble

80g (2¾oz) unsalted butter, chilled
115g (4oz) plain flour
75g (2½oz) caster sugar
80g (2¾oz) whole toasted hazelnuts, almonds, or pistachios

1 Preheat the oven to 200°C (400°F/Gas 6).

2 For the filling, simply quarter the strawberries and put in a bowl with the sugar and Grand Marnier. Give it a good stir and leave to sit.

3 For the crumble, cut the butter into cubes and put in a bowl with the flour. Using your fingertips, rub together until the mixture resembles crumbs. Stir in the sugar and nuts.

4 Spread the crumble out on a baking tray and cook for 15 minutes, then give it a stir.

5 Return to the oven for a final 15 minutes, until light golden brown.

6 Allow to cool, then serve scattered over the Grand Marnier strawberries.

Hack

Make this with any fruit - it's a good way of using up those bits from the bottom of the fruit bowl that need to be eaten. You can also serve the crumbs warm with ice cream, if you have a fruit-dodger in the house.

For some reason I had it in my head this was super-healthy, until I saw the ingredients. What the hell! It's still scrummy and it has at least one of your five-a-day

Something Special

KAYE: I love the idea of it, I really do. I just love the thought of casually dropping an invitation to friends to come round for dinner. There's nothing nicer than the prospect of good company, good wine, and good food in your own home. Then reality kicks in.

I still get traumatic flashbacks from the last time I was foolhardy or drunk enough to do it. Hacking the base off a blackened filo pastry pie, trying to salvage just one layer before the filling fell out of the bottom. Picking through the remains of "roasted" Mediterranean vegetables masquerading as charcoal dog biscuits. Listening to guests gently tapping their cutlery on the table while glancing at their watches.

The thing is, I never had "go-to" recipes for such occasions so, four or five nights in advance, I'd browse cookbooks and invariably pick out dishes way beyond my ability, using ingredients I'd never heard of. By the time the evening rolled around, I'd be in a blind panic fantasizing about breaking my leg so I could call everyone up and cancel.

But this old dog is learning new tricks. I have tried all these recipes several times and, because Nadia has anticipated the places that a Disaster Chef might go wrong and given a heads-up on what to do when, I am pleased to report that the Adams kitchen is open for business again. Last time I had friends round, I even produced a mighty fine-looking, marshmallowy pavlova. You should've seen their disbelieving faces!

Pea & Bacon Soup

Serves 4

NADIA: This could have gone in the Something Up Your Sleeve chapter (see p174–91), as everything comes out of the cupboard or freezer. But it's posh, so we put it here. Bet you wish you weren't a veggie, Kaye.

Actually it's just as nice without bacon, and your arteries will thank you for it!

- 30g (1oz) unsalted butter
- 4 spring onions, chopped
- 500g (1lb 2oz) frozen petits pois (not garden peas, see p127)
- 500ml (16fl oz) vegetable stock, plus extra if needed
- 1 tbsp lemon juice, or to taste
- pinch of sugar, or to taste
- salt and freshly ground white pepper
- 6 rashers of smoked streaky bacon (optional)

So you can't see it in the soup, but use black pepper if that's what you've got

1 Melt the butter in a large saucepan over a low heat (use a heat diffuser here, see p13). Add the spring onions and cook until softened but not coloured.

2 Tip in the petits pois and stock, and bring to the boil, then reduce the heat and simmer for about 5 minutes, or until the peas are tender.

3 Using a blender or a hand-held blender, whizz until smooth (only half-fill the blender and be careful, as hot soup scalds). Add more stock if you'd like a thinner soup.

4 Stir in the lemon juice, sugar, salt, and pepper, then taste and adjust all these seasonings to taste.

5 Grill the bacon (if using) until nice and crisp. You can do this ahead of time and keep it on a piece of kitchen paper, so it stays crisp.

6 Ladle the soup into 4 warmed bowls and crumble over the crispy bacon.

As long as you haven't got Kaye coming over

Good Old Prawn Cocktail

Serves 4

NADIA: Don't anyone *dare* say anything about this classic 1970s-style photo. I love it. That right there is exactly what I imagine when I dream of prawn cocktail. It's the law. None of your fancy-pants updating-with-fruit-and-crayfish for me.

- 2 Little Gem lettuces
- 500g (1lb 2oz) cooked prawns
- 10 heaped tbsp mayonnaise
- 2 tbsp tomato purée
- 4 tsp Worcestershire sauce
- 2 tsp Tabasco sauce
- 2 tbsp lemon juice
- salt and freshly ground black or white pepper
- 4 tsp chopped chives, to garnish
- 1 lemon, cut into 4 wedges, to serve

1 Separate the lettuces into leaves and divide them equally between 4 martini glasses. (The tacky cocktail glass is a must!)

2 Sprinkle the prawns over the top.

3 Mix the mayonnaise, tomato purée, Worcestershire sauce, Tabasco sauce, lemon juice, salt and pepper in a bowl. Check the seasoning, then spoon the sauce over the prawns.

4 Finish with the chives and lemon wedges.

Do this sparingly – you don't want the prawns swimming in sauce

Smoky Fish & Beet Pâté

Serves 4

NADIA: This is the best thing ever. I've been quite conservative with the horseradish because I know some people fear it (naming no names, Kaye). So feel free to add more if you want extra kick. I do!

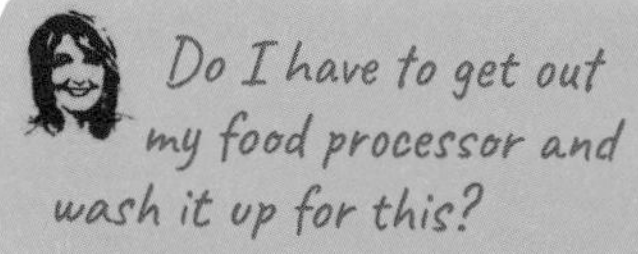

No, you can just break it all up with a fork if you prefer a rougher pâté

- 3 smoked mackerel fillets, about 250g (9oz) in total
- 125g (4½oz) cream cheese or crème fraîche
- 2–4 tsp creamed horseradish
- zest and juice of ½ unwaxed lemon, or to taste
- 2 cooked beetroot, about 100g (3½oz) in total

Taste and see if you want more

To serve

- toast or oatcakes
- watercress
- lemon wedges

1 Remove the skin and any bones from the mackerel, and put the flesh in a food processor with the cream cheese or crème fraîche, horseradish, lemon zest, and juice.

2 Pulse until you have a pâté of the consistency you prefer.

3 Finely chop the beetroot and stir into the pâté to get a beautiful colour. Taste; you may want more lemon juice or more pepper (you probably won't need more salt). Serve with toast or oatcakes, watercress, and lemon wedges.

Feta & Pepper Filo Pie

Serves 4

KAYE: Dare I say that Ms Sawalha has come up with a stroke of genius here? I love filo pastry but all that layering it and mucking about puts me off. By just scrunching balls of filo on the top, it's so much easier, but still looks really impressive. And, let's face it, it's nice to turn out something that good-looking. It makes a change from people asking, suspiciously, "What is it?"

2 red peppers, deseeded
2 green peppers, deseeded
2 yellow peppers, deseeded
2–3 tbsp olive oil
2 onions, sliced
4 garlic cloves, crushed
salt
1 tsp dried oregano
20 black olives, pitted
400g (14oz) feta cheese
4–5 sheets of filo pastry
knob of unsalted butter, melted
1 tbsp sesame seeds

1 Preheat the oven to 180°C (350°F/Gas 4).

2 Slice all 6 peppers into even-sized chunks rather than long slices. Set aside.

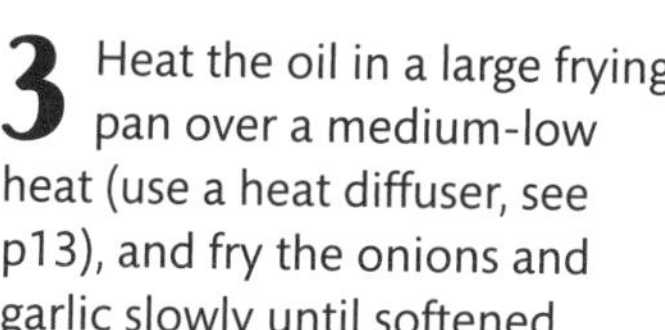

3 Heat the oil in a large frying pan over a medium-low heat (use a heat diffuser, see p13), and fry the onions and garlic slowly until softened.

4 Add the peppers and a good pinch of salt, reduce the heat, and cook for 5–8 minutes, or until softened.

Take your time, the peppers will soften and, as they do so, become sweeter

5 Stir in the oregano and olives. Transfer the mixture to an ovenproof dish and crumble over the feta cheese. Leave to cool so the pastry doesn't melt.

How will I know what size dish to use?

Any in which the filling makes a good satisfying layer; reckon on about 20cm (8in) square or the equivalent

Continued >>

6 Tear the filo sheets in half and place them under a clean, damp tea towel. Brush each piece of filo with melted butter, then scrunch them up and top the pie with them.

Why do I need to put the filo under a shroud?

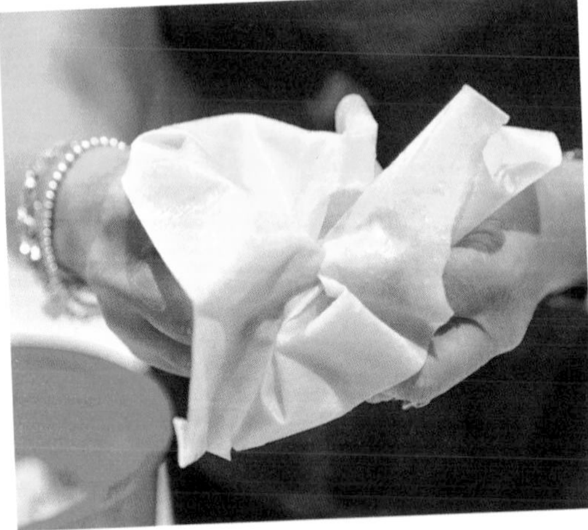

Because otherwise filo will start to dry up and crack – you also need to work quite fast here

7 Sprinkle evenly with the sesame seeds and a little more salt. Put in the oven for 15–20 minutes, or until golden and crisp. Serve warm.

HACK

You can use pretty much any vegetable here, instead of, or as well as, peppers. Try aubergines, courgettes, or spinach.

Whole Baked Red Snapper

Serves 2–4

NADIA: If you can't find red snapper, just use any whole fish – sea bream is always good cooked whole – choosing whichever looks freshest. But get the fishmonger to gut it. Life's too short to do that yourself.

2–4 large red snapper (depending on size and people's appetites), cleaned and gutted

salt and freshly ground black pepper

1 small bunch of parsley, half left as whole sprigs, half with the leaves stripped and finely chopped

1 small bunch of lemon thyme, half left as whole sprigs, half with the leaves stripped

finely grated zest and juice of 1 unwaxed lemon

1 tbsp olive oil, plus extra for drizzling

8–10 garlic cloves, crushed

8 tomatoes, halved

What's the cavity?

The bit inside where the guts came from – stuffing herbs here will flavour the fish from the inside out

1 Preheat the oven to 200°C (400°F/Gas 6).

2 Pat the fish dry with kitchen paper and season with salt and pepper inside and out. Fill the cavities with most of the parsley and thyme sprigs.

3 In a small bowl, mix together the chopped parsley leaves, the thyme leaves, the lemon zest and juice, and the oil and garlic.

4 Using a sharp knife, make 2 slits on either side of each fish, through the thickest part.

Why do I need to assault the fish?

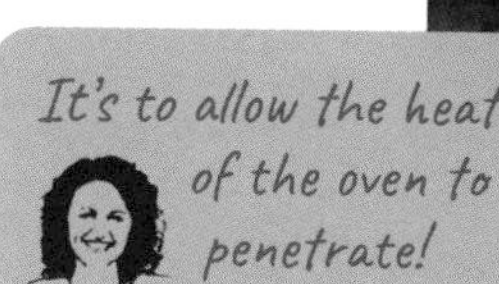

It's to allow the heat of the oven to penetrate!

5 Fill the slits in the fish and their cavities with the chopped herb, lemon, and garlic mix. Push some of the remaining herb sprigs into the slits, too.

6 Lay the fish on a baking tray with the tomatoes around them. Sprinkle with the remaining herb sprigs and drizzle the tomatoes and fish with olive oil. Season the tomatoes very well with salt.

Continued >>

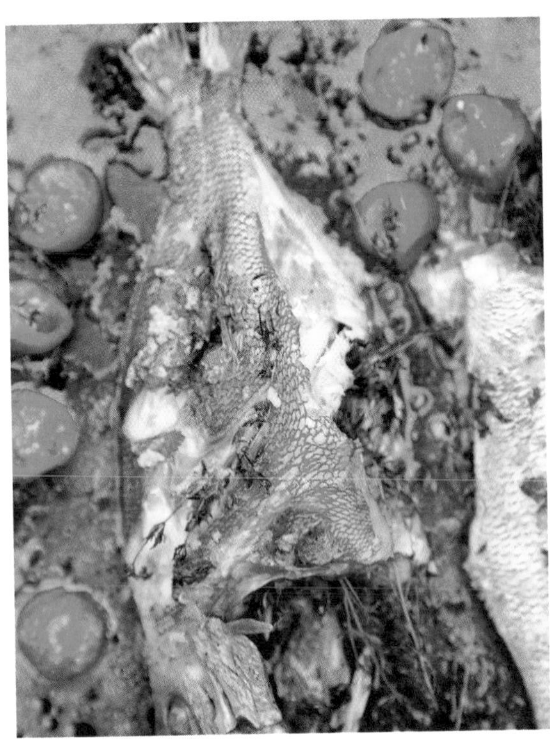

7 Put into the oven for 25 minutes, or until cooked through.

How will I know when the fish is cooked through?

The flesh flakes when you press on it with a fork – you can feel it coming away from the bones

8 Either serve 1 snapper per person or, if you used 2 large fish, cut each in half in whichever way seems fairest to you, and serve.

FAFF ALERT

I would definitely finish off the fish under a hot grill for a bit of crispiness, but Kaye would rather grill herself than bother with this.

Watch out where the fish bones end up – they're dangerous for dogs

Coq au Riesling

Serves 4

KAYE: This is a bit of a French fancy. It has loads of flavour from the dried mushrooms, which are a handy storecupboard ingredient as they instantly perk up most casseroles. If you really want to impress your guests, serve this while wearing a string of onions round your neck. And a beret, of course.

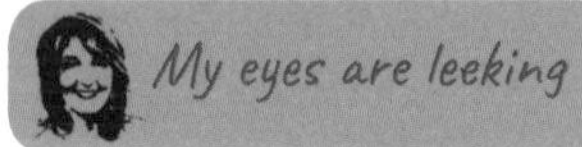

- 3 leeks, really well washed
- 150g (5½oz) smoked bacon lardons
- 30g (1oz) unsalted butter
- 8 skinless and boneless chicken thighs
- 600ml (1 pint) Riesling
- 3 bay leaves
- 30g (1oz) mixed dried mushrooms, soaked and drained
- salt and freshly ground black pepper
- 6 tbsp double cream

Soak according to packet instructions

To finish

- 1 tbsp olive oil
- 1 garlic clove, crushed
- 200g (7oz) your favourite fresh mushrooms, quartered
- handful of parsley leaves, finely chopped

1 Chop the leeks into 4cm (1½in) pieces. Set aside.

You need to wash leeks between their layers to remove soil – yes, it's tedious

Please don't do what Disaster Chef is doing here: do not use a metal spoon in a non-stick pan or you'll damage the pan

2 Place a large, heavy-based frying pan over a medium heat and throw in the lardons. Fry until just turning brown, stirring the whole time.

3 Reduce the heat and add the butter and leeks. Stir for a minute, then reduce the heat again and let the leeks soften for another minute.

4 Add the chicken and give it a stir, then pour in the Riesling and bring it up to a good bubble.

5 Let the liquid reduce a little, then reduce the heat and add the bay leaves and soaked and drained dried mushrooms. Season well with salt and pepper.

Not the first time I've seen Nadia reduce a pint of Riesling

Nor the last – in fact, great idea Kaye, cheers!

Continued >>

6 Cover the pan and simmer very gently for 30 minutes, or until the chicken is cooked through.

Cut into a thick piece to check there's no trace of pink

7 Stir in the cream.

8 To finish, heat the oil in a clean frying pan over a medium-high heat, add the garlic and let it sizzle, then throw in the fresh mushrooms, parsley, and plenty of salt and pepper.

9 Stir briskly for a couple of minutes, then scatter on top of the chicken.

10 Serve with boiled new potatoes, rice, flat noodles, or simply with some rustic bread and petits pois.

HACK

Make this with bone-in chicken pieces if you want, to add more flavour, but cook for 45 minutes.

White Choc & Berry Cheesecake

Serves 8

KAYE: I love this because I don't have to bake it! So easy: naughty, but not too sweet, as the lemon juice adds a good kick. I admit I have never successfully completed it because I eat all the ingredients before I get to the making part. Some might call it gluttony; I call it time-efficiency.

- 100g (3½oz) unsalted butter, plus extra for greasing
- 200g (7oz) digestive biscuits
- 500g (1lb 2oz) full-fat cream cheese, at room temperature
- 30g (1oz) icing sugar
- finely grated zest of 1 unwaxed lemon
- 50ml (1¾fl oz) lemon juice
- 100g (3½oz) white chocolate, broken into pieces
- 300ml (10fl oz) double cream
- 50g (1¾oz) raspberries

Hack

Don't let any moisture get into the chocolate or it will seize up and you'll have to throw it away. Even a wooden spoon can hold moisture and ruin your chocolate - metal spoons only!!

Just stick the chocolate in the bloomin' micro!

1 Lightly butter a 20cm (8in) round springform tin, then line the base with baking parchment.

2 Put the biscuits in a food processor and blitz until they're fine crumbs, or put them in a bag and bash with a rolling pin. Melt the butter in a small saucepan over a medium-low heat, pour it into the crumbs and mix until biscuit and butter come together. Press into the tin with the back of a spoon and put into the fridge.

You can either bring the biscuits up the sides or have a thicker base: up to you

3 Put the cream cheese, icing sugar, lemon zest, and juice into a bowl, and whisk until smooth.

4 Place the chocolate in a heatproof bowl and set it over a saucepan of barely simmering water (don't let the bowl touch the water). When the chocolate is nicely melted, let it cool for a couple of minutes. Briskly fold it into the cream cheese mixture until well combined.

Why can't the bowl touch the water?

Because the chocolate will seize if it does, it needs to have indirect heat only

5 In a separate bowl, whip the cream until soft peaks form, then gently fold into the chocolate mixture. Pour over the biscuit base and smooth it out, again with the back of a spoon. Cover and chill overnight.

6 When you're ready to serve, remove the cheesecake from the tin, put it on a plate, and arrange the raspberries around the edge of the cheesecake.

Marshmallowy Fluffy Pavlova

Serves 6–8

NADIA: Right, trust me. You *can* make a perfect pav, one with a light, crisp shell and a soft, marshmallowy middle. Just follow this recipe word for word, take heed of my warnings, and you will taste true culinary success. If I look the worse for wear in these photos, it's because I was!

For the meringue

2 tsp raspberry vinegar or white wine vinegar, plus extra for cleaning the bowl

lemon juice, for cleaning the bowl (optional)

4 large egg whites, at room temperature

225g (8oz) caster sugar

2 level tsp cornflour

For the cream

350ml (12fl oz) double cream, chilled

1 tsp vanilla extract (optional; don't worry if you haven't got any)

2 tbsp icing sugar, sifted (optional), plus extra for dusting

For the topping

blueberries, raspberries, and strawberries

1 On a large piece of baking parchment, draw around a 23cm (9in) dinner plate with a pencil. Turn the parchment over so it's pencil-side down and place on a baking tray. Preheat the oven to 150°C (300°F/Gas 2).

2 Clean a large glass or metal bowl with a little bit of vinegar or lemon juice.

Odd as it sounds, acid will clean away any trace of fat in your bowl: fat is the enemy of stable egg whites, if it's there, they won't whip up!

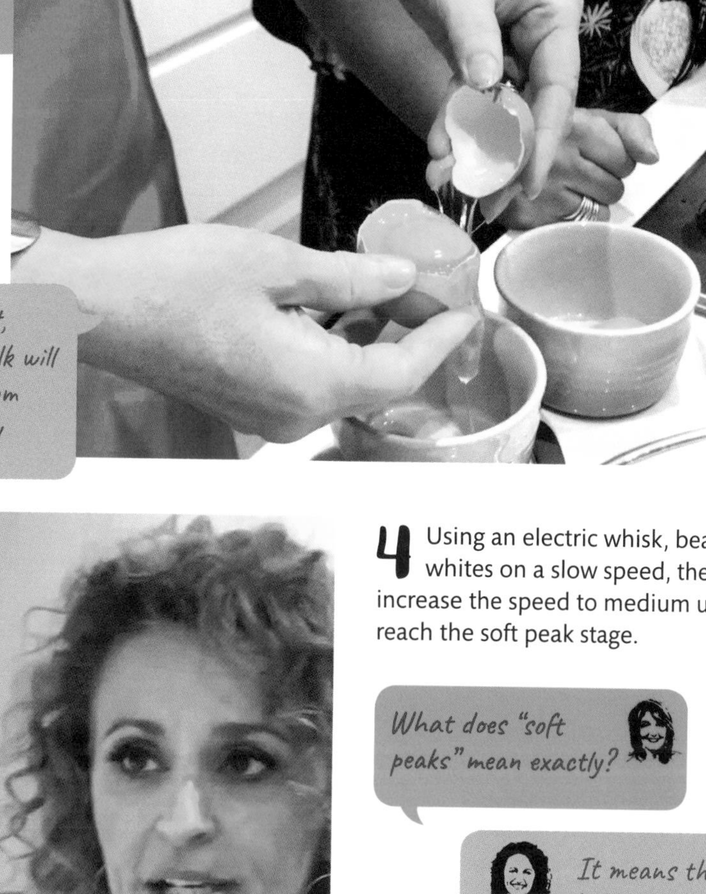

3 Separate the eggs, ensuring the whites are completely free of yolk. Pour the egg whites into the super-clean bowl.

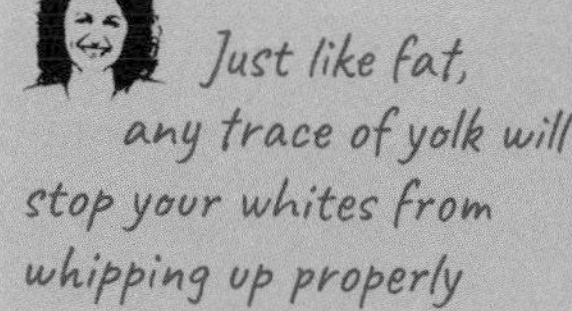

Just like fat, any trace of yolk will stop your whites from whipping up properly

4 Using an electric whisk, beat the egg whites on a slow speed, then gradually increase the speed to medium until they reach the soft peak stage.

What does "soft peaks" mean exactly?

It means that, if you hold your whisk upside-down, the peaks of the mixture will just hold their shape before flopping down

5 Increase the speed of the whisk to its highest, then, whisking continuously, add the sugar, a spoonful at a time, until the meringue is shiny and the sugar thoroughly mixed in. If you were to hold the whisk upside-down now, the meringue would stand up in proud (stiff) peaks.

Continued >>

6 In a cup, whisk together the vinegar and cornflour until smooth. Whisk this mixture into the meringue.

7 Spread the meringue to fill the baking parchment circle, building up the sides so that they stand higher than the middle. Place in the oven and bake for 1 hour. Once baked, turn off the oven and leave the door ajar. Leave the pavlova inside the oven until it has cooled completely. This stops it from cracking.

I had to concentrate so hard the first time I made this, I considered crushing two paracetamol into it. I didn't. It was worth it

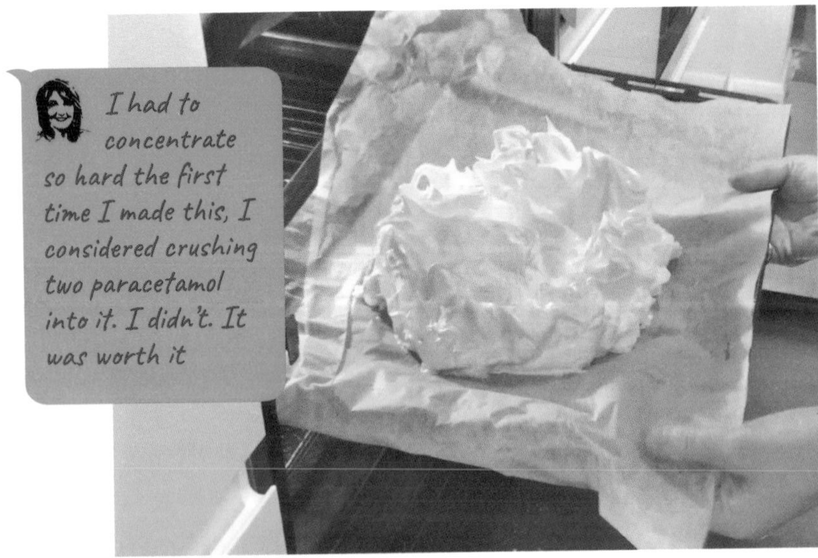

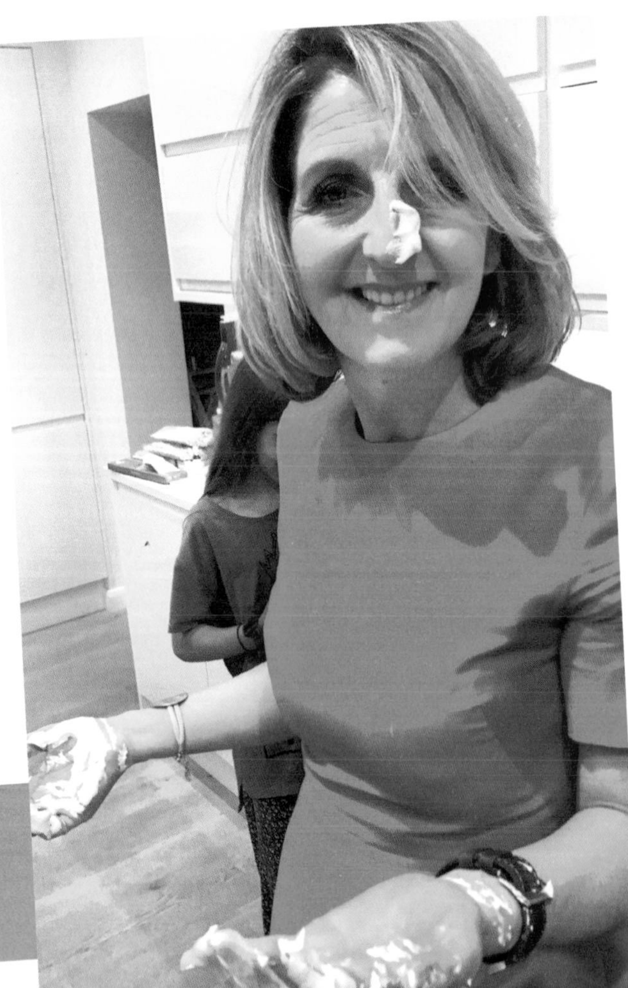

8 Combine the chilled cream with the vanilla extract and icing sugar (if using) in a large bowl. Beat on a low setting using an electric whisk, then gradually increase the speed to medium and whisk just until the cream increases in volume and begins to stiffen, but still has soft peaks. Dollop the cream into the centre of the cooled pavlova.

I'm talking cream straight from the fridge here

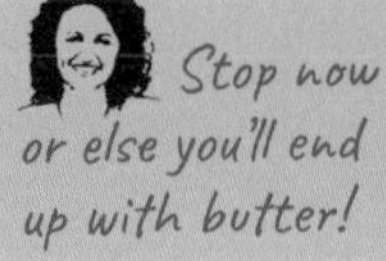

9 Scatter the blueberries, raspberries, and strawberries over the cream and dust with icing sugar. Ta-Dah!

Another way of testing the stiffness of your meringue mix: dollop some on your nose

Index

A

B

C

D

E

F

G

H

I, J

K

L

M

N

O

P

Continued >>

Editors: Lucy Bannell, Amy Slack
Editorial assistant: Rosamund Cox
Designers: Hannah Moore, Philippa Nash
Recipe tester: Elizabeth Bray
Photographer: Mark Adderley
Managing editor: Stephanie Farrow
Managing art editor: Christine Keilty
Senior pre-producer, production: Tony Phipps
Senior producer: Stephanie McConnell
Art director: Maxine Pedliham
Publisher: Mary-Clare Jerram

First published in Great Britain in 2018 by
Dorling Kindersley Limited
80 Strand, London WC2R 0RL

A Penguin Random House Company
10 9 8 7 6 5 4 3 2 1
001–309995–Mar/2018

A CIP catalogue record for this book is available from the British Library.

ISBN: 978-0-2413-3773-8

Printed and bound in Slovakia

A WORLD OF IDEAS:
SEE ALL THERE IS TO KNOW

www.dk.com

And now for the Oscars...

NADIA: Oscar for Best Crap Cook goes to my wonderful friend Kaye Adams, without whom this book would have just been like every other flaming cookbook! Our friendship means the world to me, even though you are bloody annoying... G&T anyone?

Oscar for Best Husband and Photographer Extraordinaire goes to my darling Mark. Love every shot baby! You are my very own polymath! Love you forever xx

Oscar for Best Agent goes to Nicola Ibison. You are a force of nature, thank you thank you thank you! Here's to many more great books!

Oscar for Best Team Ever goes to DK's publishing director Mary-Clare Jerram and her crazy brilliant crew... thank you so much, you lovely lot.

Oscar for Best Foodie Mum in the world goes to Betty. If it wasn't for you I'd never have written a single recipe. Love you x

KAYE: If anyone had told me a year ago that I'd ever put my name to a cookbook, I'd have laughed them out of town. But thanks to those marvellous mavericks at DK and our ever-optimistic agent, Nicola Ibison, Disaster Chef is born.

This project has been a joy and a pleasure to be involved with and I will ever be grateful to Nadia and Mark for doing the lion's share of the work, while I coped with a personal annus horribilis. I could not wish for truer friends. They make me laugh, they let me cry, and they feed me into the bargain.

My wonderful Mum, Cathie, cannot go without mention. She made me the crap cook I am today so, without her, this book would never have happened. Thanks also to my long-suffering partner Ian and my beloved girls, Charly and Bonnie, for all the times you've reassured me, "No, really, it's nice."

Nadia & Kaye

Best friends and television presenters Nadia Sawalha and Kaye Adams are well-known for being panellists on the long-running ITV daytime chat show *Loose Women*.

Nadia originally rose to fame as an actress, appearing as Annie Palmer in the BBC's *EastEnders*, and later went on to win *Celebrity MasterChef* in 2007. This is her sixth cookbook. Kaye, meanwhile, is a highly respected journalist and broadcaster, having made her name reporting current affairs for ITV and STV. She currently hosts a daily radio show for BBC Scotland.

Together, the pair host their own YouTube channel, **Nadia & Kaye**, where they vlog about a range of subjects, including cookery, parenting, and "menopausal moments".

Find Nadia and Kaye online:

YouTube: www.youtube.com/c/nadiaandkaye

Facebook: @nadiaandkaye

Instagram: @nadiaandkaye

Twitter: @nadiasawalha and @kayeadams